JUDY FLORENCE

Creative Designs

FOR HAND AND MACHINE QUILTING

EZ INTERNATIONAL

Editing by Mary Coyne Penders.
Technical editing by Darlene Zimmerman.
Book and cover design by Kajun Graphics, San Francisco.
Diagrams and quilting by Judy Florence.
Computer graphics by Kandy Petersen, Moraga, California.
Photography by Sharon Risedorph, San Francisco.
Author's photograph by Dave Florence.

Printed in Hong Kong.

First edition.

Library of Congress Cataloging–in–Publication Data

Florence, Judy, 1945–
        Creative Designs for Hand and Machine Quilting

        1. Quilting—Designs   2. Quilting—Techniques   3. Crafts and Hobbies

ISBN 1-881588-17-3

EZ International
95 Mayhill Street
Saddle Brook, New Jersey 07663

Dedication

To Dick, Matt, and Dave, the men in my life, with affection.

Acknowledgments

I AM HONORED to acknowledge the following women, whose quilting designs have been adapted to include in this book. I appreciate their willingness to share their creations for our use and enjoyment.

Thanks to each of you for your consent and cooperation.

Anderson, Linda E.
Anderson, Linda L.
Anderson, Sally B.
Backhaus, Barb
Barnes, Sheila Mahanke
Bjerkaas, Jude
Blakely, Elaine
Boutte, Yvette
Bronson, Ann
Burdsall, Sue
Campbell, Darlene
Drewsen, Sherry
Fitzpatrick, Jackie Putnam
Foye, Mary E.
Fry, Janet Reifler
Gilbertson, Kay A.
Graham, Susan M.
Harrison, Jackie
Hayden, Betty
Hayden, Patti
Henley, Jennifer B.
Hudock, Gretchen Kluth
Hyatt, Midge
Jannausch, Betty
Jensen, Marge
Johnson, Helen
Kassera, Doris
Kirchner, Elizabeth

Koser, Renae E.
Lane, Beth Restrick
Lee, Patricia Gammon
Leland, Donna
Lipp, Robin
Loomans, Kathleen E.
Marxen, Patsy
Mattson, Ann
Michaels, Lorraine
Misiak–Davis, Kathryn
Murphy, Mary Lynn
Narotzky, Terri
Natzic, Patricia L.
Pelto, Julie C. Brownlee
Peters, Kathy
Phillips, Doris A.
Poulter, Pat
Rutland, Charlotte Lapington
Schmokel, Dawn Faulkner
Seeley, Cindy
Switzer, Peri Irish
Trask, Shirley A.
Valenta, Carol A.
Webert, Nancy
West, Karen
Williams, Daphne
Wright, Charlotte
Zinn, Judith Allen

Preface

I SPENT A GOOD PORTION OF LAST WINTER on a self-imposed quilt sabbatical. I did two things. I put down my thimble, to let it cool down, and I turned off the word processor, for the same reason. Then I allowed myself such favorite indulgences as putting jigsaw puzzles together (from my substantial collection of puzzles with quilt designs), pleasure reading (usually curled up near a toasty wood fire), playing the piano (my major mid-life financial investment was an upgrade from a studio to a grand), and probably most important, ice-skating (to the refrains of Beethoven's Third and Seventh symphonies).

The sabbatical seemed to work. I became absorbed in the relaxation of reading and puzzling, and in the rhythm of music and skating. It was a welcome respite from a world saturated with quilting and writing. Our neighborhood skating pond is within view of my quilt room, and it was very convenient for me to don my skates and wander across the street for uninterrupted skating solitude. Icy cold mornings usually brought a fresh delicate layer of frost on the pond, and sometimes a thin layer of new-fallen snow. I skated across the surface of ice in giant circular patterns, caught up in the motion of the exercise and the rhythm of the music. I would fill the entire icy surface with flowing lines and curved patterns. My mind and body, through music and exercise, became rested and comfortable.

Eventually it occurred to me what I was really doing was making giant quilting designs on the ice. As I skated, I was creating dozens of figures and miles of curves and circles similar to what I often do with needle, thimble, and thread on fabric. The parallels were clear. Most of a gnawing cold January (winter in northern Wisconsin can be brutal) passed with a sense that I was getting more than a much needed sabbatical from quilting and writing, and much needed exercise. I had skated miles of circles and figures, and through entire scores of symphonies, creating patterns all along the way.

I found myself comfortably captured in this routine of creative loafing—reading, jigsaw puzzling, playing the piano, and ice skating. I was reveling in my winter of renewal when on the last day of the month a flag went up. I received a call from my editor, inquiring about the status of this manuscript. I admitted to my self-imposed sabbatical and reiterated my intentions to get going on the manuscript. The next day would bring a flip of the calendar page and a perfect opportunity to add segments of serious writing and quilt designing to my winter routine. So a timely telephone call became the signal for me to move on, to bring my respite from quilting and writing to a close, and set my pen to paper once again.

Weeks and seasons have passed, and I no longer have crisp cold air to refresh my senses, nor a glassy pond upon which to etch arcs and curlicues. However, I have made a natural transition from my ice skates to a new pair of in-line skates, and now I am caught up in the rhythm of in-line skating, once again creating circular patterns and designs. Almost on a daily basis, you can find me somewhere in the neighborhood forming both fresh and familiar shapes with my skates. Sidewalks, streets, and parking lots have become like pages in a sketch pad as I fashion imaginary patterns. Although they leave no visible markings, these designs and movements bear an undeniable resemblance to quilting. Once again I detect the likeness between movements of body, arms, and legs and the lines and motions of quilting designs.

Now summer has come and gone. I have adapted some of those skating patterns into quilting designs. In other less obvious ways, the rhythm and lines of skating have been transformed into creative quilting designs for you to use and enjoy.

Preparation of quilting designs and diagrams for a book manuscript is a time-consuming task. I've been working on it during the transitional periods between the seasons suitable for ice skating and in-line skating. It appears that I will get this manuscript completed just in time to dust off the ice skates and move on to Beethoven's Fourth and Eighth.

Judy Florence

Table of Contents

Introduction

Since I began to teach quiltmaking almost twenty years ago, I have presented a conglomeration of classes, workshops, and seminars. Of the many topics and techniques offered, my workshop titled *How to Create Your Own Quilting Designs* remains among the most enduring and requested. What began as a modest series of paper and pencil exercises has evolved into an impressive workshop that combines technical experiments, a clinic, and portfolio designs.

Enthusiasm and satisfaction usually run very high among the participants in this workshop. The key factor in their satisfaction is the realization that they can create their own quilting designs! And once they have experienced success and satisfaction, they are enthused about making more designs and using them in their quilts. The combination of success and satisfaction leads to confidence for these quiltmakers.

My earliest creative quilting designs came during my medallion phase. Several of my medallion quilts were based on a central motif, with various sets and multiple borders. The spaces between cried out for quilting. I needed designs to fit specific and often peculiarly-shaped spaces, and I needed motifs compatible with the medallion designs. What I found in books and magazines was not suitable. To maintain the integrity of the medallion quilt, I needed custom-made designs. Thus began my first attempts at creating my own quilting designs.

This book is divided into three large sections. The first is the **Workshop** section, in which I lead you through exercises to introduce you to the basic elements and preparation for design. I give examples of **Designs,** with detailed step-by-step diagrams, so you can see how they came into being. This is not a mysterious process, and I have made every effort to clarify techniques along the way. Every design is presented full size and ready for your use.

Following the designs and their accompanying diagrams, you will have the opportunity to experiment. Each chapter has a **Now It's Your Turn!** section with a **Workpage** providing space for you to try the technique just previously explained and illustrated. This is your chance to quiz yourself on a particular technique and to make your own designs.

Section Two highlights several **Special Techniques,** where in-depth design procedures are explored. Here you learn to unlock the secrets of positioning, design extraction, continuous line designs, interlocking patterns and transferring designs. You also discover secondary designs and simple tactics to set designs into motion. Each process is illustrated with thorough diagrams and completed designs.

The third portion of the book is the **Portfolio** section, which includes twenty-two full size ready-to-use designs for blocks, backgrounds, and borders. A variety of sizes and styles, including classics, flora and fauna, and innovative designs are included. Together with the seventy-nine full size designs in the **Workshop** and **Special Techniques** sections and the five Oversize Patterns in Appendix F, you will be equipped with 106 previously unpublished quilting designs, suitable for both hand and machine quilting.

One of my primary goals is to help you visualize quilting designs in their formative stages. I encourage you to open your eyes, and I show you what to look for. This builds confidence for creating your own designs.

Here's another way to describe the contents and purpose of this book. Most quilt books devote very little thought and space to the selection of an appropriate quilting design. They devote even less thought and space to the individual creation of a quilting design. A book or chapter typically concludes with "and then quilt it". *Creative Designs* is the book that fills that large gaping void.

This book is more than just a batch of easy-to-trace lovely designs. It emphasizes the steps that lead up to the designs, presented in a workshop format. You will see the process, and try the process. All of the quilting designs are a bonus.

It is my sincere hope that you will "enroll" in the workshop. By doing so, you can experience the achievement and satisfaction of creating your own quilting designs.

Workshop PREPARATION AND PROCEDURES

SUPPLIES: A DOZEN ESSENTIALS

THE NUMBER OF SUPPLIES required for making quilting designs is minimal. No major expenditure is necessary. You probably have most of these items around the house.

Although many of these supplies are everyday items, certain features and details are desirable. I will comment on some of the specifics of each item and list some good choices. I will also share my personal preferences and reasons for my selections.

1 SHARP PENCILS OR MECHANICAL PENCILS

Sharp No. 2 pencils or fine point mechanical pencils are best for making quilting designs. Either a 0.5 mm or 0.7 mm mechanical pencil will do. My personal preference is a 0.5 mm clicker style automatic pencil. It produces a smooth, crisp line which is easy to apply and easy to erase. Keep an adequate supply of refill lead on hand. If pencils are your choice, be sure to have a pencil sharpener too.

2 ERASER

A separate eraser is more convenient for the exercises in this book. An art gum style, or a white or light-colored eraser work well. I favor a clicker style white eraser. It makes a clean, smooth, and thorough removal of pencil lines. It can be advanced and retracted as needed, and lasts a long time. Most styles also are refillable, so they are worthy of the investment.

3 PAPER

Two kinds of paper are needed:

• A quadrille pad (graph paper) marked with 4 squares per inch (2.5 cm). A pad of 8½ by 11 inch (21.6 by 27.9 cm) graph paper works best for doing the exercises in this book.

• Unlined white paper.

For making your own designs for your quilts, white unlined paper works best. The white paper should be lightweight and easy to mark and erase. Typing paper, computer paper, freezer paper (the dull side), clean newsprint, or non-adhesive shelf paper are all possibilities. White tissue paper is too fragile, and construction paper is too coarse. Something between these two would be suitable.

4 SCISSORS

You won't need your special fabric scissors. A scissors for cutting paper and template material will do. You may also find a small scissors with sharp points useful for trimming the fine details and rounding the curves on templates. I use an inexpensive pair of regular scissors (7 inch [17.8 cm]) for the paper patterns and a small scissors (4 inch [10.2 cm]) for trimming templates.

5 FINE-POINT BLACK MARKING PEN

A fine-point or extra-fine marker is best for making your designs. Avoid using markers that make a thick line. Black is best because it gives a high contrast graphic mark.

When patterns are highlighted with a fine, broken black line, they resemble the quilting designs in a style we are accustomed to seeing. Precision point rolling ball pens also work well. I prefer a black extra-fine rolling ball pen.

6 RULERS

The minimum requirement is a set of three:

6 inch (15.2 cm)
12 inch (30.5 cm)
18 inch (45.7 cm)

Clear (see-through) rulers work the best for making designs described in this book. Rulers with ⅛ and ⅟16 inch markings (or with millimeter markings) are helpful. If they have a beveled edge, that is also convenient, but not a requirement.

My favored rulers are an inexpensive set of three clear rulers that I found in the school supplies section of a variety store. They are marked with inches on one edge and centimeters on the other.

All the measurements in the book are given in both inches and centimeters. If you need clarification about conversion from one system to the other, please refer to the Metric Conversion Chart in Appendix D at the back of the book.

7 TEMPLATE MATERIAL

Durable plastic is the best choice. It should be transparent (clear) or translucent (partly transparent). Template plastic with graph lines is suitable because the lines can double as guidelines for positioning templates for tracing.

Cardboard or other opaque materials are less suitable because you can't see through them. What is being covered is always a mystery. It is helpful to be able to see through the templates to properly position them and create the most effective designs.

My favorite material for templates is lightly shaded thin plastic, similar to the kind used for x-ray film. The blue or gray shading is light enough to see through. The shading also has a cumulative effect when templates are overlapped. This allows me to see newly formed designs, created in an even darker shade, when templates are combined.

8 PENCIL OR PEN FOR MARKING TEMPLATES

Look for a marker that leaves a permanent, non-smear mark on the plastic. You probably have one on hand. Test it on your template material to see if it makes a permanent line that does not smudge. Some suitable markers are wax based, others are felt-tip style. The one I am currently using is a permanent laundry marking pen. Be careful not to use this pen in unintended places. I do not recommend using the same marker for both your templates and your designs (#5 above). They are two separate supplies.

9 BOTTLE OF WHITE CORRECTION FLUID

A small bottle of correction fluid will be necessary when you begin to highlight your designs with the black marking pen. An eraser is useless then. The correction fluid corrects errors or decision changes. One wonders how we got along without this stuff.

I also use a white fluid correction pen. It is convenient for small changes and corrections in the designs.

10 PLASTIC TRIANGLE

A large clear triangle is convenient for making large squares, triangles, and corners for border patterns. A T-square ruler could also be used. The triangle should have a 90 degree corner and 45 degree angles. In addition to the 90/45/45 triangle, a triangle with a 90 degree corner and 60 and 30 degree angles may be useful.

11 PROTRACTOR

Don't panic. It's that plastic half–moon shaped gadget. You probably have one tucked away in some drawer with old school supplies. A few of the exercises in the book are crafted from angles other than those formed from just horizontal, vertical, and diagonal lines. The protractor helps you find those measurements, and opens the door to creation of quilting designs in all sorts of divisions.

12 COMPASS

It's the two–legged device that makes circles—sharp point on one leg, pencil or marker on the other leg. A compass is helpful not only in delineation of circular spaces, but also for making hexagons and other polygons. Have one handy, just in case.

SIMPLE SHAPES, INTRICATE DESIGNS

MANY INTRICATE CLASSICAL DESIGNS are based on the simplest of elements. Successful designers have proven over and over again that a complicated motif is not necessary to create effective designs. Quite the opposite is true. A simple, unadorned shape is often the basis for elegant designs.

The quilting designs in this book are based on one of three basic shapes—a teardrop, a heart, and a flower. Some are based on a combination of these basic shapes. None involves any motif more complicated than these three. In fact, one of the best guidelines for creating your own quilting designs is to start with a simple motif.

In the **Workshop** section of this book, I will guide you through step-by-step procedures for creating the designs. Beginning with a simple shape, I will illustrate preparation, positioning, and discovery of new quilting patterns. I invite you to work (or is it play?) along with me in this process so you can understand more fully the step-wise nature of emerging designs. Then you can forge ahead with confidence and make your own personal designs, using the guidelines and spaces I have provided for you.

Teardrops

WE BEGIN with the teardrop shape. The beauty and versatility of the teardrop lies in its combination of both curved and angular lines within a small space. The gently rounded end is balanced by the sharply pointed end. We have the best of both worlds—curved and angular—within a compact shape. When we make multiple images of the teardrop, lovely patterns that capitalize on these gentle curves and sharp points are born.

In order to effectively illustrate the step-by-step process of creating designs for quilting, some of the diagrams and illustrations are reduced in size. Using reduced size examples allows me to fit more diagrams on a page, and allows you to see the design progression more readily. In all instances, however, there is a full size illustration of the completed design—ready for you to use in your own quiltmaking projects. You may find it helpful to follow along in the procedure by making your own full size

pattern, using the given dimensions and actual templates.

The choice of size for the teardrop depends mainly on the space for which you are planning your design. Most of the designs in this book are based on a small teardrop (about 2¼ inches [5.7 cm] long) or a large teardrop (about 3¼ inches [8.2 cm] long). We can easily make designs for a variety of sizes of blocks and spaces with these two teardrops. Spaces as small as 3 inches (7.6 cm) in width and height, and as large as 15 inches (38.1 cm) can be accommodated.

 ## Challenge

If you are working with very small spaces (e.g., in miniature quilt designs, or compact locations such as corner squares in lattice work), you may need to use an even smaller teardrop. I have provided a pattern for a tiny teardrop that measures 1½ inches (3.8 cm) long, which should be more suitable. For very large spaces (e.g., alternate plain blocks or whole cloth quilts), an extra large teardrop may be required. The pattern for a 4¼-inch (10.8 cm) teardrop is also provided. Select the size that best suits your quilting style.

TO MAKE DESIGN #1

The first step is preparation of the template. Refer to the teardrop templates on page 189.

1. Make a clear plastic template of the 2¼-inch (5.7 cm) teardrop. Be sure to center and mark the horizontal and vertical guidelines (looks like a cross) with a template marker. Trim the point

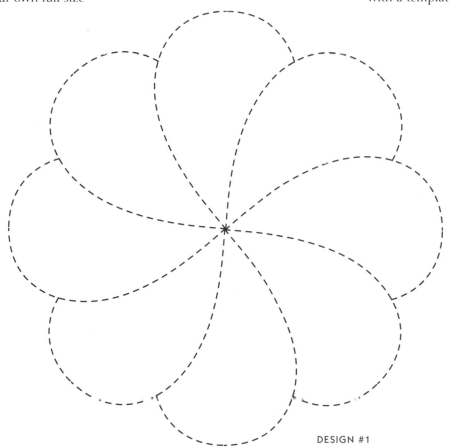

DESIGN #1

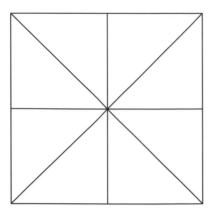

Diagram 1

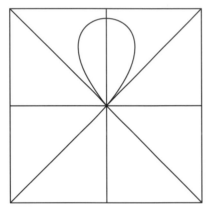

Diagram 2

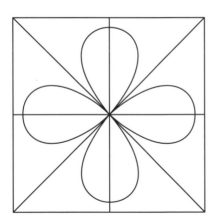

Diagram 3

of the template so it is sharp, and cut the curved edges smoothly.

2. Begin with a 5-inch (12.7 cm) square. To locate the center point, simply fold it into fourths and lightly mark the horizontal and vertical lines. (Don't forget to use a sharp pencil, mark lightly, and keep an eraser handy!) To make the diagonal divisions, mark lightly from corner to corner. The prepared square is shown in Diagram 1.

3. Place the small teardrop with the point at the center of the square, and the rounded edge toward the top of the block. Use the vertical line on the template as a guide and position it directly over the vertical line on the square.

4. Trace lightly around the teardrop (Diagram 2). Similarly, place the teardrop in the other vertical and horizontal positions (toward the bottom and toward the sides) and trace lightly around the teardrop. The result is a clover-like figure, as shown in Diagram 3.

5. To complete the elements of the design, place the teardrop on the diagonal lines. Place the point at the center of the square and match the vertical line on the template with the diagonal lines on the square, as in Diagram 4.

6. The next step involves removal of excess lines. In this example, lines are removed for two reasons. The first is to reduce congestion in the center. There are too many lines (sixteen) coming together in the middle. If all the lines were actually stitched into the quilt, the result would be a mass of unsightly stitches and a flattening of the area. It would become over-quilted. Removal of every other line segment (marked with an X in Diagram 5) solves the problem.

The second reason to remove some of the lines is to add a sense of motion. Removal of the above mentioned line segments accomplishes this. Once the line segments have been erased, what is otherwise an entirely symmetrical, stationery design begins to revolve in a circular fashion, as shown in the final illustration of Design #1.

7. Darken the final shape with black broken lines. This highlights the design and also makes it feel more like a quilting design. I suggest using a fine or extra-fine point felt-tip black marker. Rolling ball markers also work very well.

8. Remove all the horizontal, vertical, and diagonal pencil guidelines from the background. Erase any other excess or unused pencil lines. Design #1 is now complete and ready for use.

Diagram 4

Diagram 5

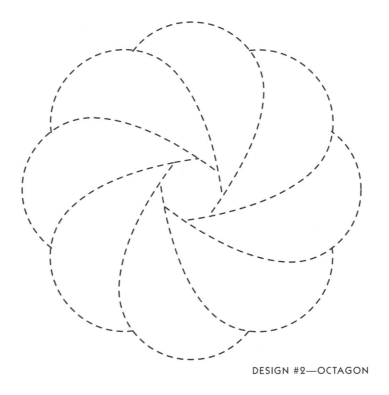

DESIGN #2—OCTAGON

TO MAKE DESIGN #2

This design also features the tear-drop in a radiating format. This design differs mainly in the placement of the teardrops. The teardrops overlap one another, resulting in a more snug or compact design. There is also a sensation of more intense swirling from the center.

1. Begin with a 4-inch (10.2 cm) square. Locate and mark the quarter sections and diagonal lines by folding and drawing in pencil lines, just as in the previous design. Instead of using the center as the focal point, mark dots $\frac{1}{2}$ inch (1.3 cm) from the center, in all directions (horizontal, vertical, and diagonal), as shown in Diagram 6.

2. Position the teardrop as before, with the rounded end toward the top and the pointed end near the center. This time the point will overlap the center line. Place the point on the dot and match the line on the template with the vertical line on the square. Trace lightly around the teardrop, as in Diagram 7.

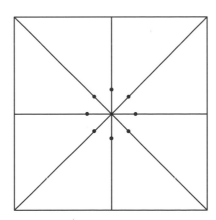

Diagram 6

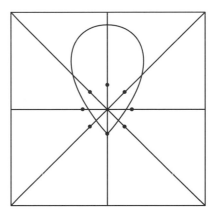

Diagram 7

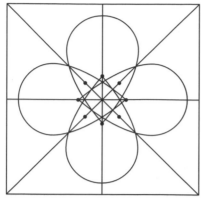
Diagram 8

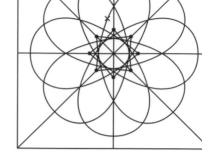
Diagram 9

3. Add the other three teardrops at the bottom and sides, as in Diagram 8.

4. Place the remaining four teardrops on the diagonal lines, with the pointed ends overlapping the center of the square and positioned on the dots. Lightly trace around them. The result will be a circular design with many (too many!) intersecting lines in the center (Diagram 9).

5. Remove selected line segments (marked with an X) to reveal the spinning floral design.

Darkening the remaining curved lines until they intersect with the next adjoining teardrop results in a central octagon (8–sided figure). This is an effective secondary design, which I personally think makes it more attractive. If you are uncomfortable with the prospect of stitching this small octagon, now is the time to reach for your loose change, find a nickel, place it in the center, and trace around it. Design #2, with either a circular or octagonal center is ready for your use.

DESIGN #2—CIRCLE

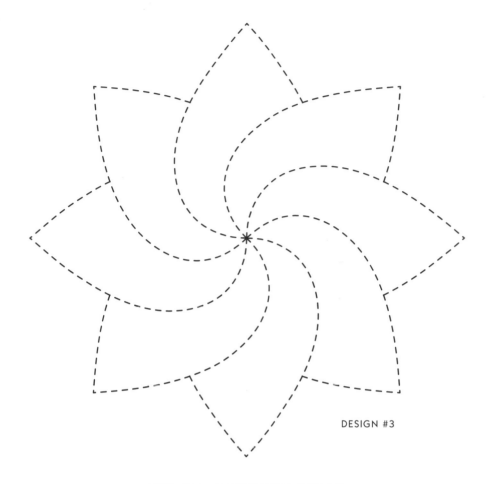

DESIGN #3

TO MAKE DESIGN #3

An entirely different effect is accomplished when the teardrop is rotated and placed with the curved end toward the center and the pointed end radiating outward. Design #3 features this opposite placement.

1. Begin with a 5-inch (12.7 cm) square. Locate and lightly mark the horizontal, vertical and diagonal lines, as in Diagram 10.

2. Position the teardrop with the rounded end at the center of the square and the pointed end toward the top, matching the vertical line on the template with the vertical line of the square. Lightly trace around the teardrop. Similarly, place the teardrop in the other three positions and trace, as in Diagram 10.

3. Continue with placement on the diagonal lines, with the rounded end at the center and the pointed end toward each corner of the square. Diagram 11 reveals the results.

4. Many design options are lurking about in this square. For now, we will

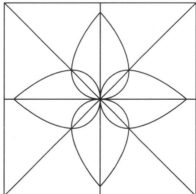

Diagram 10

Diagram 11

settle on a simple one that parallels our earlier design (#1). This helps you see the effective difference between placement of the teardrop with points in and points out. Remove line segments marked with an X to reveal a more effective, less frenetic design.

5. Darken the pattern with black broken lines to complete Design #3, a swirling, double pinwheel pattern, now ready for your use.

✿ Challenge

If, at this point, you detect other designs within Diagram 11, you are well on your way to becoming a proficient and prolific designer! (You'll have a real adventure when we get to the section on *Design Extraction*). Study Diagram 11 to discover other attractive designs. Search for other shapes and patterns. Then finger trace them on the Diagram. You may want to isolate and trace these found designs for future use.

TO MAKE DESIGN #4

Design #4 is made in a procedure similar to Design #3. The primary difference is that this new pattern is more compact, with teardrop shapes that overlap in their placement.

1. Begin with a 5-inch (12.7 cm) square. Draw in the usual horizontal, vertical, and diagonal lines to divide the space into equal size workable areas.

2. Rather than using the center as the focal point, mark locater dots ¼ inch (.6 cm) from the center, on all eight lines (Diagram 12).

3. Next, place the teardrop with the pointed end toward the top of the square, and the rounded end overlapping the center line, and positioned on the marked dot. Trace around it. Position the template in the other three vertical and horizontal positions and trace around them, as in Diagram 13.

4. Next, place the teardrop along a diagonal line, with the pointed end toward the corner and the rounded end positioned on the dot. Lightly trace around the teardrop. Repeat in the other three corners, as shown in Diagram 14.

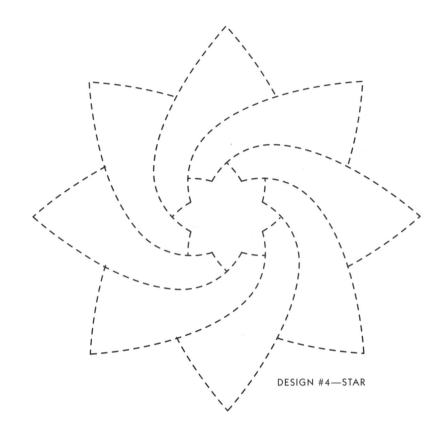

DESIGN #4—STAR

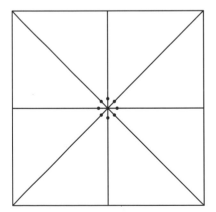

Diagram 12

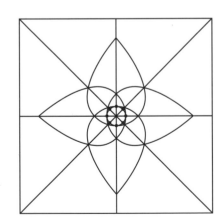

Diagram 13

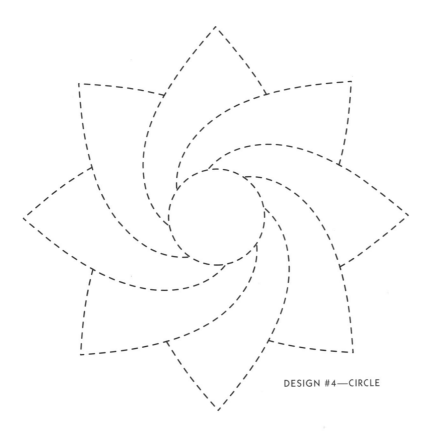

DESIGN #4—CIRCLE

5. Erase selected line segments (marked with an X) and excess lines in the center of the square to reveal the star flower in the center (Diagram 15).

6. Darken in the final design with broken lines. An optional circular center may be used for Design #4. Simply substitute a circle (trace around a coin or a spool of thread, or use a compass) for the center star.

Part of the pleasure derived from making your own quilting designs is the surprise element—discovery of shapes and figures that were unanticipated. In the process of placing, rotating, repositioning, and superimposing, new design elements appear. These unplanned elements can become the focus of the quilting pattern. A simple secondary design may take on a life of its own and become the primary design.

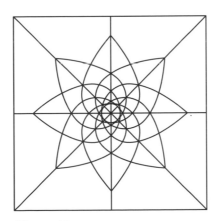

Diagram 14

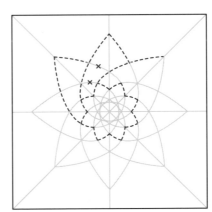

Diagram 15

TO MAKE DESIGN #5

Design #5 features secondary design elements that have become the primary design. It is made from the small teardrop template, but does not resemble a teardrop. The teardrop shape has been stripped of both its rounded curve and its sharp point. A refreshing new shape has taken its place. The steps for making Design #5 are illustrated in Diagrams 16–19.

1. Begin with a 5-inch (12.7 cm) square of paper. Divide the paper into quarters and lightly mark the horizontal and vertical lines. Measure 1 inch (2.5 cm) from the center on all four lines and mark the locater dots, as in Diagram 16.

2. Place the small teardrop template with the pointed end at the center and the rounded end toward the outside of the square, matching the lines on the template with the lines on the square. Trace four teardrop shapes (a clover-like figure), as in Diagram 17.

3. Next, rotate the teardrop so the rounded end is toward the center of the square and the pointed end is toward the outside. Position the rounded end at the locater dot and match the line on the template with the line on the square. The pointed end of the teardrop extends beyond the square. Trace around the curved end of the teardrop, up to the edges of the square (a horseshoe shape). Repeat this on all four sides, as shown in Diagram 18.

4. To highlight the design, darken in the new central shape with broken lines (Diagram 19). Finally, erase all excess lines and pencil guidelines from the background.

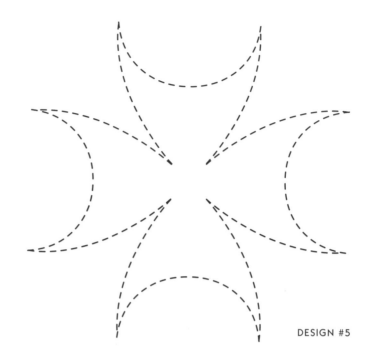

DESIGN #5

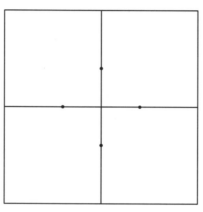

Diagram 16

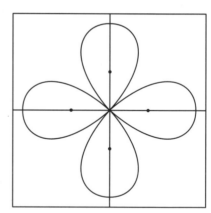

Diagram 17

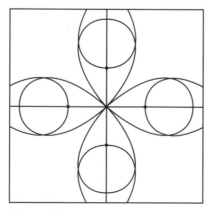

Diagram 18

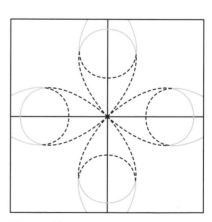

Diagram 19

TO MAKE DESIGN #6

This design differs mainly in its ori-entation. It is set on point rather than on edge. The curves seem more gentle and the angles are less penetrating. The steps for making Design #6 are shown in Diagrams 20–24.

1. Begin with a 5-inch (12.7 cm) square. Lightly mark the diagonal lines. Add locater dots ¼ inch (.6 cm) and 1 inch (2.5 cm) from the center on each line, as in Diagram 20.

2. Place the small teardrop along the diagonal line, with the rounded end toward the corner and the pointed end overlapping the center, at the ¼ inch (.6 cm) dot. Trace around the teardrop, as shown in Diagram 21. Likewise, position the teardrop toward the other three corners and trace lightly around it, as in Diagram 22.

3. Next, rotate the template and place it with the pointed end toward the corner and the rounded end on the outer locater dot. Trace around the template. Do the same in the other three corners, as shown in Diagram 23.

4. Highlight the new design with dark broken lines, as in Diagram 24.

5. Finally, erase all excess lines and diagonal guidelines to reveal Design #6.

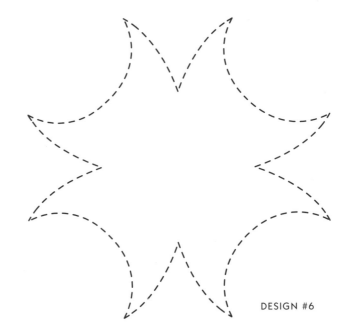

DESIGN #6

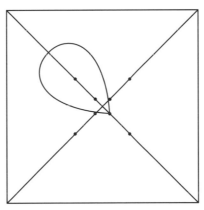

Diagram 21

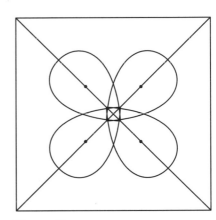

Diagram 22

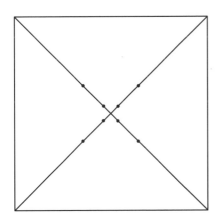

Diagram 20

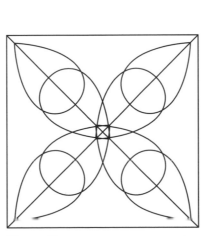

Diagram 23

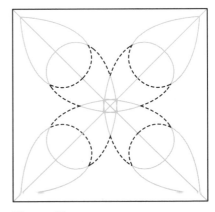

Diagram 24

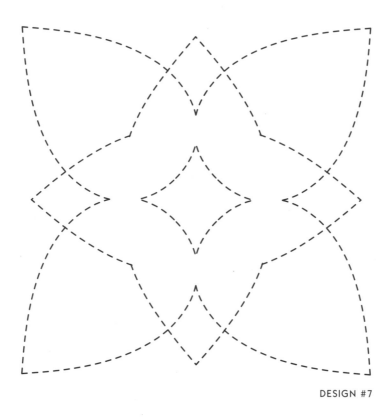

DESIGN #7

TO MAKE DESIGN #7

Secondary design elements play an obvious role in Design #7. Once again only the small teardrop is used. How it is positioned and rotated determines the final simplicity or complexity of the design. Brand new floral and celestial shapes are suggested. The steps for making Design #7 are shown in Diagrams 25–29.

It requires the same number of teardrop images used in the previous designs.

1. Begin with a 4–inch (10.2 cm) square. Pencil in the horizontal, vertical, and diagonal guidelines. Add locater dots ¼ inch (.6 cm) from the center on the diagonal lines. On the horizontal and vertical lines, mark dots ½ inch (1.3 cm) from the center, as in Diagram 25.

2. Position the teardrop template with the pointed end toward the top and the rounded end overlapping the center line. The teardrop should touch the locater dot, as shown in Diagram

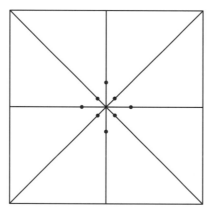

Diagram 25

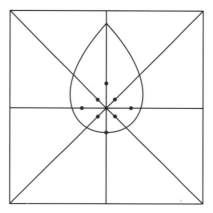

Diagram 26

26. Trace lightly around the template. Add three more teardrops that point toward the sides and bottom of the square, as in Diagram 27.

3. Place the second set of teardrops with the pointed ends toward the corners of the square, as in Diagram 28. Be sure to place the rounded end at the locater dot and match the line on the template with the diagonal line on the square.

Diagram 28 offers multiple design choices. Clearly, if all the lines were left in, there would be too many crowded lines, too many intersecting lines, and undesirable congestion. I have chosen to highlight the floral images that radiate from the center, as in Diagram 29. Removal of other extraneous lines, leaving only the 4–pointed star in the center and the larger 4–pointed star in the background, results in a reasonable amount of quilting, and an attractive design.

Diagram 27

Diagram 28

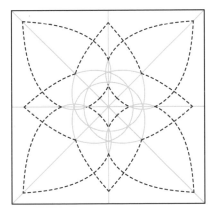

Diagram 29

✤ *Now it's your turn!*

Several sections of this book include **Workpages** for you to try a new technique on your own. Full size squares are provided so you may work directly with the templates on a prepared space.

If in reading and studying the seven designs in the previous section you detected other patterns, if you think there were better choices, if you saw something I missed, or if you think you can improve on any of the designs, now is the time and here is the place to experiment. My observation in workshops has been that my students often outshine the instructor, and I continually see fresh, innovative designs making their way onto paper. I wish I could witness your creative adventure.

Don't forget to gather the necessary supplies before you begin:
- Sharp pencil
- 6-inch (15.2 cm) clear ruler with inch and centimeter markings
- ¼ inch (.6 cm) graph paper
- plain white paper
- clear plastic for templates
- pen or pencil for marking templates
- eraser
- scissors

The teardrop template is provided in four different sizes on page 189. I recommend using the small one (2¼-inch [5.7 cm]) on the **Workpage** (see next page). If you elect to use a smaller or larger teardrop, then you may need to prepare smaller or larger background squares.

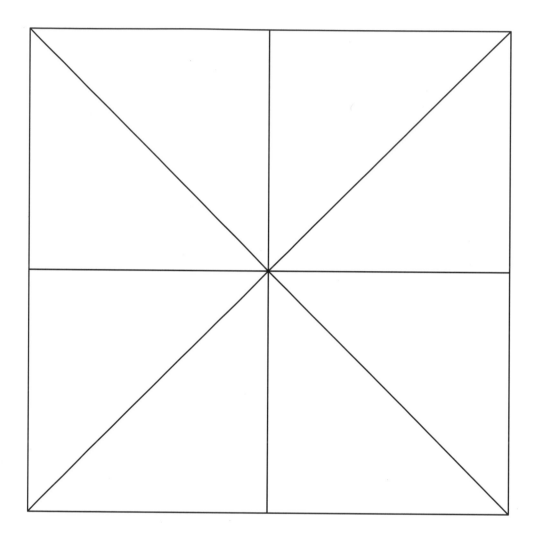

DESIGN #8

T HE HEART parallels the teardrop in its possession of appealing elements—gentle curves and penetrating angles. The heart offers additional design features —an indentation (concave dip at the top of the heart) and a mirror repeat of the curved area. We discover more patterns with fewer images.

TO MAKE DESIGN #8

This design is a simple arrangement of overlapping hearts.

1. Begin by making a clear template of the medium–size heart on page 190. Make the edges as smooth as possible and add the centering line on the template.

2. Make a 5-inch (12.7 cm) square.

Lightly mark the diagonal lines. Mark locater dots 1 inch (2.5 cm) from the center along the four diagonal lines, as in Diagram 30.

3. Place the heart template with the pointed end toward the corner and the indentation at the locater dot. Trace lightly around the heart (Diagram 30).

4. Repeat the heart image in the

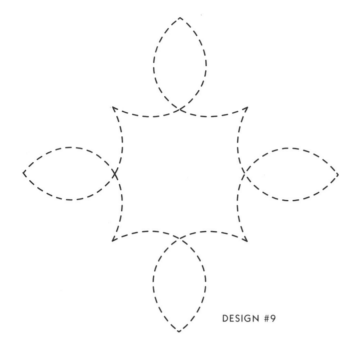

DESIGN #9

other three corners, as shown in Diagram 31.

5. Use a fine point black marker to darken in the broken lines of Design #8.

6. Erase the diagonal guidelines and outer edges to reveal the completed design.

Yes, this is an elementary placement concept and a simple arrangement. But the result is undeniably suitable for quilting—not too many lines, not too few—sufficient lines to declare the space adequately quilted.

 Challenge

For the ten percent of the quilting world (that's my own estimate) that claim an aversion to hearts, don't skip this section. You may be pleasantly surprised at the variety of designs that can be derived from the heart. Challenge yourself to make at least one heart design that pleases you.

TO MAKE DESIGN #9

The bonus of Design #8 is the lovely secondary design in the center of the square. Removal of the outer areas of the heart, as shown in Diagram 32, reveals Design #9—a compact, continuous line figure suitable for small spaces such as corner squares or the background areas in pieced and appliquéd blocks.

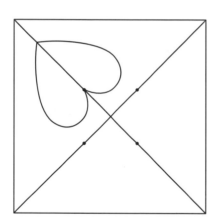

Diagram 30

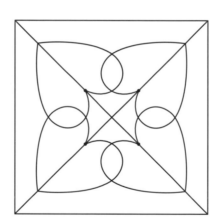

Diagram 31

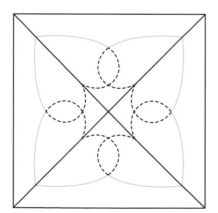

Diagram 32

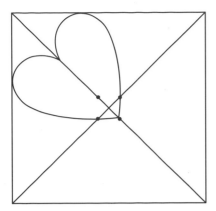

Diagram 33

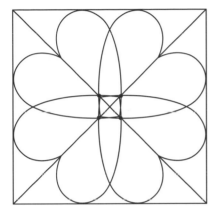

Diagram 34

TO MAKE DESIGN #10

Let's explore what happens when the heart is rotated. This design features the placement of hearts with the tips toward the center and the curved portions toward the corners of the square.

1. Begin with a 4–inch (10.2 cm) square of paper. Lightly mark the diagonal lines and four locater dots ¼ inch (.6 cm) from the center, as in Diagram 33.

2. Position the heart template with the rounded edges toward the corner and the tip overlapping the center and touching the locater dot. The curved portions of the heart should just touch the edge of the square, as in Diagram 33.

3. Continue with the placement of the hearts in the other three quadrants and trace lightly around them, as in Diagram 34.

4. Darken in the heart shapes with broken quilting lines and erase the diagonal guidelines to reveal Design #10—a combination of flowing outer curves and an inner secondary design that resembles the traditional *Crossed Canoes* pattern.

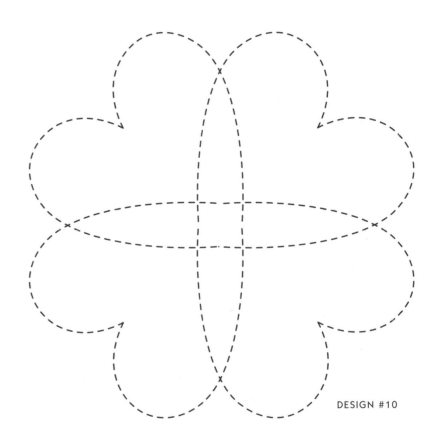

DESIGN #10

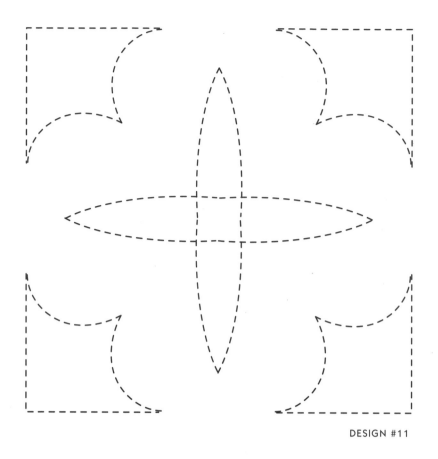

DESIGN #11

TO MAKE DESIGN #11

For an alternative view of Design #10, we can highlight the negative space created by the overlapping hearts.

1. Refer again to Diagram 34. Rather than highlighting the heart shapes, let's emphasize the center cross and the corner figures.

2. Remove some portions of the heart to reveal the hidden design elements, as shown in Diagram 35.

3. In addition to the portions of the heart template, Design #11 also employs the outer edges of the square as part of the pattern. Use your ruler and black marker to complete the straight lines at each corner.

4. Erase the unused curves and diagonal lines to complete Design #11.

A direct comparison of Designs #10 and #11 shows the dramatic difference between positive and negative space. One design feels and looks very much like the hearts from which it is composed. The other bears little resemblance to a heart. The difference is mainly one of emphasis of foreground versus background, and connected versus separated elements.

Both designs are suitable for quilting. The mechanics of stitching Designs #10 and #11 are different. Continuous line quilters may favor #10, which can be completed in one uninterrupted line of stitching. Design #11, by contrast, requires more start and stop stitching, or at the very least, some passing through of the needle from one design element to the next.

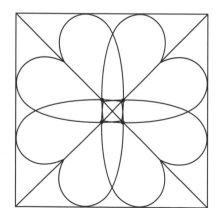

Diagram 34

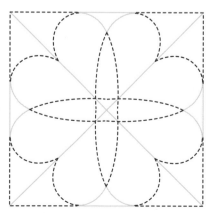

Diagram 35

DESIGN #12

TO MAKE DESIGN #12

Let's continue with a larger space and somewhat more elaborate pattern.

Design #12 uses the same small heart template, but with a total of twelve images.

1. Begin with a 6-inch (15.2 cm) square of paper. Mark the horizontal, vertical, and diagonal lines. Mark locater dots 1 inch (2.5 cm) and 1³/₄ inch (4.5 cm) from the center on the horizontal and vertical lines. Mark locater dots ¹/₂ inch (1.3 cm) on the diagonal lines, as shown in Diagram 36.

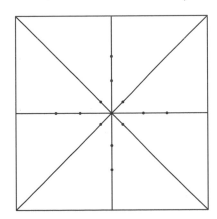

Diagram 36

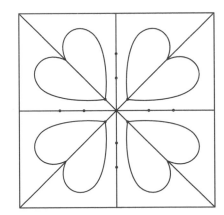

Diagram 37

2. Position the heart template along the diagonal line, with the rounded end toward the corner and the tip at the dot, as shown in Diagram 37. Place and trace around the heart in the other three corners as well.

3. Rotate the heart and position it along the vertical and horizontal lines, with the tip toward the outside of the square and the rounded end toward the center. Place the indentation of the heart at the inside dot (1 inch [2.5 cm] from the center), as in Diagram 38. Similarly, position the heart along the other three lines.

4. The final heart images are also placed along the horizontal and vertical lines, with the indentation of the heart at the outer dot, as in Diagram 39. Notice that the heart template extends beyond the edge of the square. You need only trace around the portion that covers the square. Trace the heart in all four positions—top, bottom, and both sides.

Diagram 40 reveals the highlighted Design #12—a blend of loops, curlicues, and the suggestion of *fleur-de-lis*. The heart is no longer the primary visual element. New shapes and lines have overtaken it.

 ## Challenge

Numerous strong design elements remain to be discovered in Diagram 39. Why not make a copy of it, and then take your marker in hand and see what other shapes you can find? Look in the center for radiating patterns. Look along the outer edges for elements that project into the corners. Look for stars, arrows, scallops, crosses, and other transformations of the heart.

 ## Now it's your turn!

Now that you've seen the step-by-step process of designing with the heart template, you should have increased confidence to try some of your own. Three different heart sizes are provided on page 190.

The **Workpage** includes a square prepared for design. The medium-sized heart is easiest to use. If you prefer to work on a smaller or larger space, then one of the other sizes will be more appropriate. Cut and prepare your preferred size square.

Make your heart template from clear plastic.

Now place the heart template on the square and begin your own design. Rotate it, invert it, and move it around until you detect the beginning of something that pleases you. Start with an uncomplicated design, and then move on to more intricate creations.

Challenge

During my *How to Create Your Own Quilting Designs* workshops, I encourage my students in similar step-by-step processes. They are continually surprised and pleased with the new designs they uncover. However, not every attempt is successful and not every design is a show-stopper. There are occasional disappointing and dead-end designs that not even the eraser or correction fluid can rescue. You may need to start over. You may even crumple up your design and toss it in the waste container. My disappointing designs go into one of two file folders: "Designs that Need More Work" and "Rejects". Both folders are quite thick. Once in a while I browse through them with the hope that I can rescue or rework a design. Sometimes I'm successful, and sometimes I'm not. Why not see if you can redo one of your rejected designs? Your patience and effort may be rewarded in the end. Good luck in your endeavors.

Diagram 38

Diagram 39

Diagram 40

Workpage

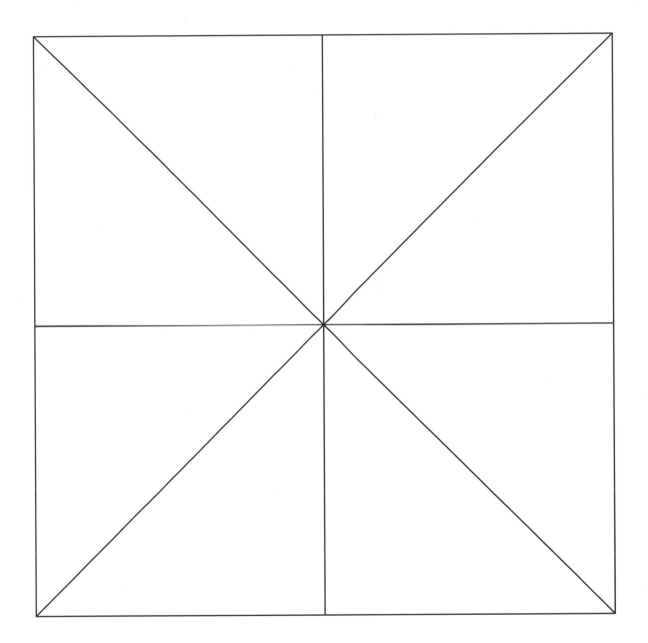

Flowers

HE THIRD MOTIF used in the quilting designs in this book is the flower. I have selected a symmetrical shape with smooth curves and gentle points. Although it is a simple figure, it surpasses both the teardrop and the heart in complexity. It has two indentations, three points, and several curved areas. The flower is a pleasing figure by itself, certainly suitable as a motif that could be multiplied and chained for lattice and border quilting patterns.

There are also several surprises lurking in this flower. When positioned flush with one another, or overlapping one another, fresh design elements appear. Expect to find things like blue-bells, poinsettias, stem-ware, birds, and crosses. When you get to the **Work-pages,** you will discover even more shapes and patterns on your own.

TO MAKE DESIGN #13

This design is a basic arrangement of four flower images.

1. Make a clear plastic template of the flower on page 188. Cut the edges as smoothly as possible, and mark the center line on the template.

2. Begin with a 6½-inch (16.5 cm) square. Mark the horizontal, vertical, and diagonal lines, as in Diagram 41.

3. Place the flower with the top toward the center of the square and the bottom toward the outer edge of the square. Move the template until the sides of the flower just barely touch the diagonal lines, and the center line matches the vertical line on the

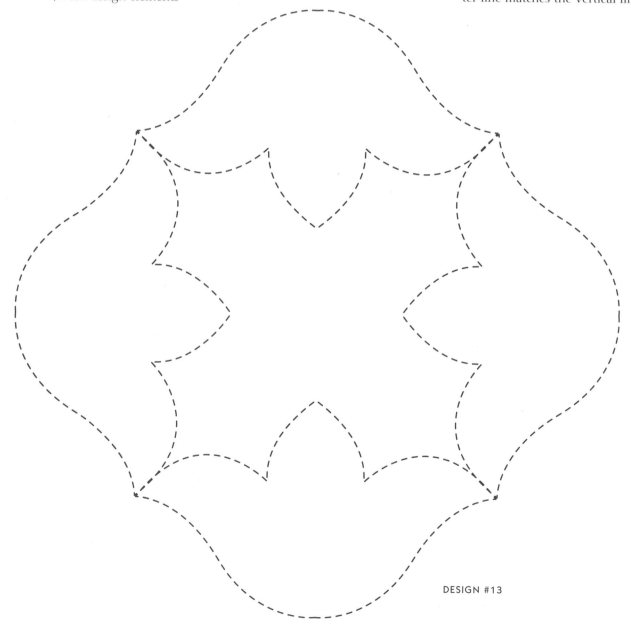

DESIGN #13

square, as shown in Diagram 41.

4. Continue by placing the flower template at the top and sides, as in Diagram 42. We can immediately detect a newly formed secondary design in the middle of the square. With its pointed leaves, it resembles a poinsettia. We can isolate and highlight just this portion, as in Diagram 42, or we can utilize the complete Design #13 as illustrated.

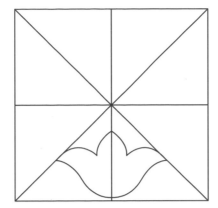

Diagram 41

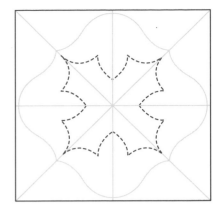

Diagram 42

 Challenge

Let's challenge ourselves to illustrate additional variations of this same arrangement of four flowers. Designs #14, #15, and #16 reveal the effect of moving the flowers closer to the center of the square. The sides of the flowers overlap and form a new curved shape in the outer corners. As the flowers move closer to the center, the inner cross is reduced and the outer motif increases in size. Diagrams 43, 44, and 45 illustrate the placement of the flowers. We have progressed from a poinsettia-like design to crosses and tulips and on to something that might resemble Aunt Grace's stem-ware. Why not try other overlapping arrangements of the flower template to discover your own designs?

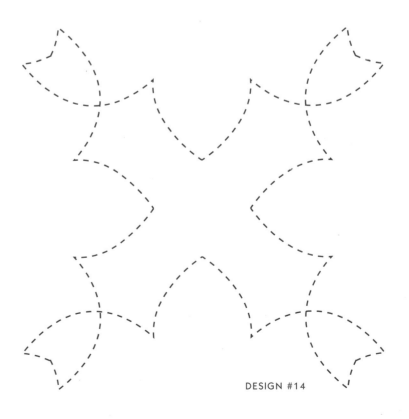

DESIGN #14

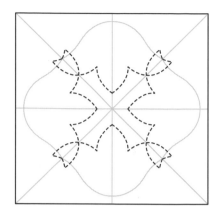

Diagram 43

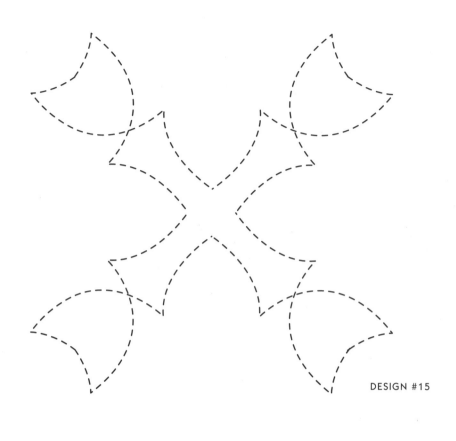

DESIGN #15

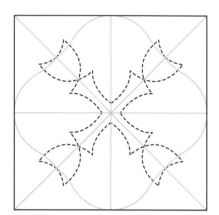

Diagram 44

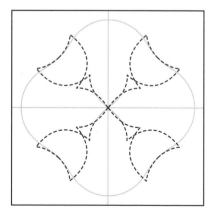

Diagram 45

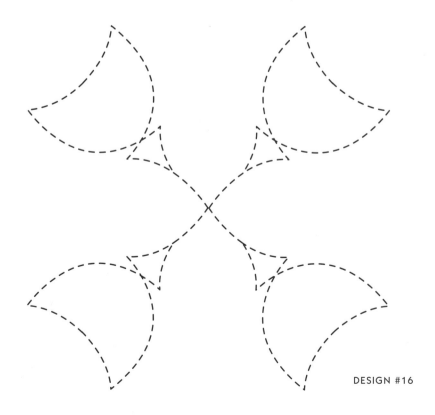

DESIGN #16

TO MAKE DESIGN #17

This design illustrates what happens when we rotate the flower template, and place the rounded end toward the center of the square, and the top of the flower toward the outer edges of the square.

1. Begin by drawing vertical and horizontal 5-inch (12.7 cm) lines that cross at the center, as shown in Diagram 46. Place locater dots 1/8 inch (.3 cm) from the center on each line.

2. Place the flower with its top pointing straight up and its bottom just overlapping the center line. The flower should just touch the locater dot and the guideline on the template should match the vertical line on the square, as in Diagram 47.

3. Next, place the template in the opposite direction (facing down), again with matched vertical lines and the lower edge of the flower at the locater dot (Diagram 48).

4. Complete the design by placing flowers along the horizontal lines, touching the locater dots and facing outward, as shown in Diagram 49.

Two new secondary designs appear– one resembles a rosebud, the other a lily or bluebell. Diagram 50 highlights these designs, either of which could be extracted and arranged in a quilting design of your own making. Removal of pencil guidelines and excess lines at the center of the block reveals Design #17, suitable for a 5-inch (12.7 cm) or larger space on your quilt.

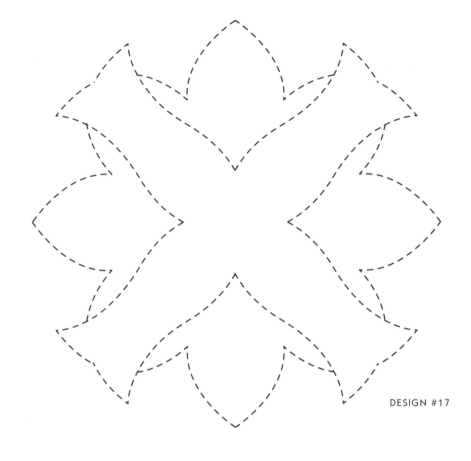

DESIGN #17

Diagram 46

Diagram 47

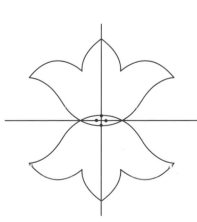

Diagram 48

Diagram 49

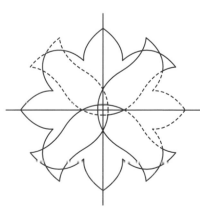

Diagram 50

TO MAKE DESIGN #18

This design is slightly more complex. The flower templates are situated in a similar manner as Design #17 (radiating from the center), but twice as many images (eight) are utilized.

1. Begin with a 6-inch (15.2 cm) square, and pencil in the horizontal, vertical, and diagonal guidelines. Add locater dots ½ inch (1.3 cm) from the center on the diagonal lines, as shown in Diagram 51.

2. Center the flower in the upper section, with the tips just touching the diagonal guidelines. Add three more floral images pointing toward the sides and bottom, as in Diagram 51.

3. The remaining four flower shapes are placed along the diagonal lines, with the bottom of the flower extending over the center of the square and touching the locater dot, as shown in Diagram 52.

4. Continue by tracing the flower image on the other diagonal lines, as shown in Diagram 53.

5. Diagram 54 includes all eight images. Removal of some of the lines from the congested area, erasure of the background guidelines, and highlighting with dark broken lines completes Design #18.

Diagram 51

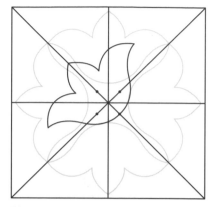

Diagram 52

Diagram 53

Diagram 54

DESIGN #18

TO MAKE DESIGN #19

A pleasant diversion awaits us in Design #19. We cross, ever so briefly, into the representational world (the real world). With just the slightest maneuver and a touch of detail, our flower is transformed into a delightful little bird, complete with beak, wing and tail!

1. Begin by drawing two lines perpendicular to each other, as shown in Diagram 55.

2. Mark a point 2 inches (5.1 cm) above the center of the square and 1 inch (2.5 cm) to the left of the center line. Draw a guideline from the center through this point.

3. Place and trace the flower template along this angle, as shown in Diagram 55.

4. Diagram 56 shows how the flower is reversed and superimposed over the first image to complete the wing portion of the bird. Add some stitching details, such as wing and tail feathers and an eye, to bring the bird to life.

DESIGN #19

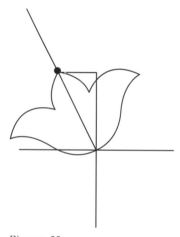

Diagram 55

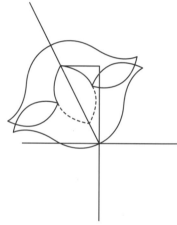

Diagram 56

 Now it's your turn!

I would like you to try two different exercises. First, make a template of the flower.

A 6-inch (15.3 cm) prepared square is provided on the **Workpage.** Place the flower template in whatever manner you want, and watch for new shapes to appear. Keep working until you have a satisfactory quilting design. Remember, it doesn't have to be elaborate.

The second exercise is an extension of Diagram 54, which by itself is a mixed-up maze of shapes and lines. I have extracted one design (#18). Study Diagram 54 to see what other designs are lurking about. There are plenty more. The easiest way to do this is to prepare your own copy of Diagram 54 by following the steps in Diagrams 51, 52, and 53. You may want to make sev-

eral copies, because you're likely to find several designs. When you find interesting shapes, bring them to life by highlighting them with dark broken lines.

If you enjoy searching for hidden designs, you can look forward to the section on *Design Extraction* later in the book. More thorough and challenging examples are included there.

Workpage

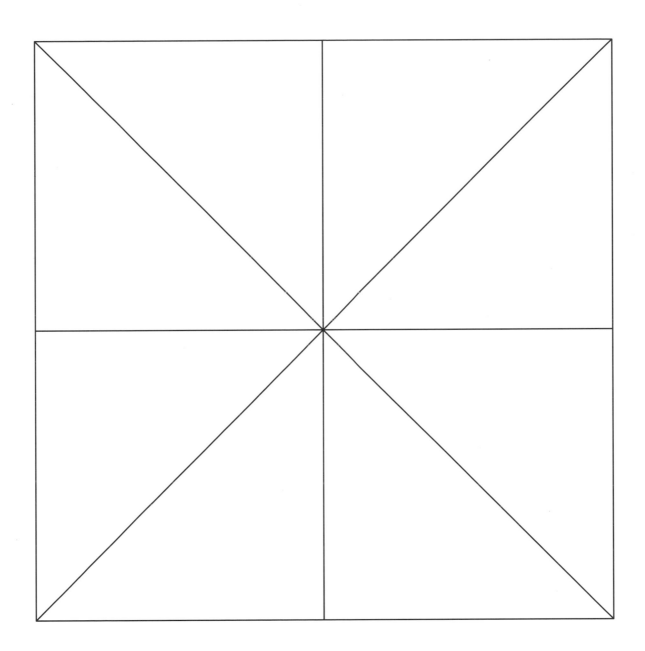

SPACES FOR DESIGNS

*I*N THE PREVIOUS SECTION we dealt with **Shapes**—the teardrop, heart, and flower. Emphasis was on the use of a simple motif to make a quilting design. Now we turn our attention to the creation of designs appropriate for specific **Spaces**—the places on the quilt surface that require quilting.

When I conduct a workshop on *How to Create Your Own Quilting Designs,* I include what I have termed a clinic portion. Participants are invited to bring in their quilt tops, incomplete works, and projects in mid–stream for which they are perplexed about how, where, and what to quilt. Together we attempt to solve the dilemma, offer advice, make specific design suggestions, and generally encourage each other with some positive choices.

Some quiltmakers often feel they have a unique or unsolvable quilting design problem. More often than not, they just need to be shown how to define the spaces, how to select a design motif, and how to integrate the quilting with the piecing and appliqué already on the surface of the quilt. Together, we can usually accomplish this in our quilt clinic.

Most of the spaces that cry out for quilting can be loosely grouped into three categories: Blocks, Triangles, and Rectangles. I have created these admittedly expansive groupings to clarify the description of the territories that need quilting.

I have chosen the word **Blocks,** rather than squares, because it is a broader term that includes not only the squares we frequently encounter in quilting, but also other closely related shapes like octagons, hexagons, circles, and less precise spaces that occur in our pieced and appliquéd quilts, such as the center of a *Double Wedding Ring.* Think of these areas as blocks of space that need quilting.

Triangle spaces refer not only to the obvious side and corner tri- angles that occur in various quilt settings, but also the pieced triangles in blocks such as *Ohio Star, Amish Shadow,* and *Snail's Trail.* Triangles also include the less definite spaces around appliqué patterns such as

Dresden Plate, Rose of Sharon, and *Grape Basket.* The concept of triangular spaces will be more fully explained in the next section.

Rectangles encompass both lattice work and borders, the two most obvious rectangular shaped spaces on a quilt. However, rectangles include even more. Consider the rectangular or elongated areas in traditional pieced patterns such as *Roman Stripe, Brickwork,* and *Log Cabin.* Extension panels and spacers often come in a rectangular format. Spaces that are longer than they are wide will be considered at the end of this section.

A special section for **Borders and Corners** has been included. Here the teardrops, hearts and floral designs are formatted for longer borders and corner treatments. These larger renditions are illustrated in the Oversize Pattern section at the back of the book.

Blocks

W HEN CONSIDERING the blocks of space that need to be quilted, we use a broad definition, including any area that is about as wide as it is long. It may be an exact square, or some other quadrilateral or polygon that only suggests or feels like a square, including spaces that are hexagonal (6–sided), octagonal (8–sided), and circular. Blocks also include diamonds that are squares set on point.

Oftentimes, a design that is intended for a square is also appropriate for a circle. Upon close examination, we find that hexagons and octagons really do read like circles. As you examine the designs in this section, notice whether or not they are presented as if quilted onto a square, a circle, or some other shape. Then try to imagine what the design would look like in a differently shaped space. You may want to make

some clear templates of various shapes, such as squares, hexagons, octagons, and circles, to help visualize how the design would fit into another space. Or have your compass handy to swing an imaginary circle over a design to see if it is suitable for a round space. In this way you can consider the versatility and multiple use prospect of each design.

This section includes several designs, from very small to quite large,

from simple to complex. All are appropriate for the blocks of space on a quilt.

DESIGN #20 rests comfortably on its 5–inch (12.7 cm) square. It would also fit suitably on squares ranging from 4$\frac{1}{2}$ to 6 inches (11.4 to 15.2 cm). Diagrams 57, 58, 59, and 60 illustrate how it would also fit other blocks of space —a square on point, a circle, a hexagon, and an octagon.

Most of the designs in the **Blocks** section pass this versatility test. They are quite adaptable to other spaces.

The basis for Design #20 is given in Diagram 61. Notice that it uses only $\frac{1}{2}$ of the teardrop in a radiating format, some from the center, others overlapping the center. Inclusion of diagonal, horizontal, and vertical line segments adds a sense of motion, and also provides its distinguishing quality.

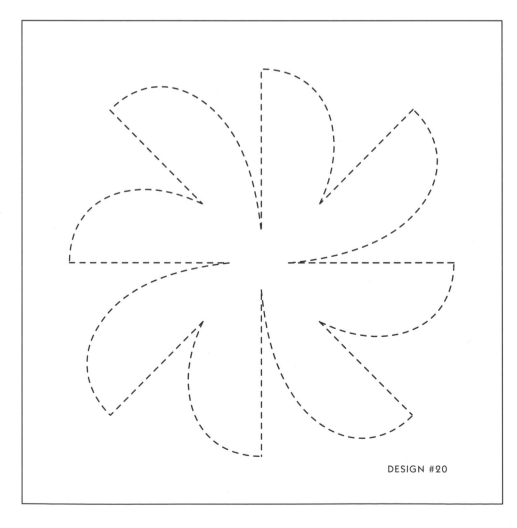

DESIGN #20

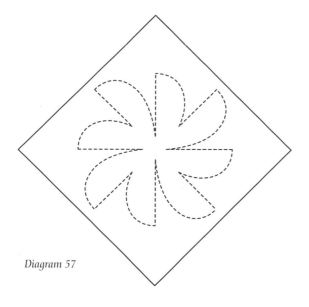

Diagram 57

Diagram 58

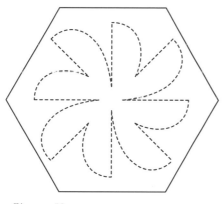

Diagram 59

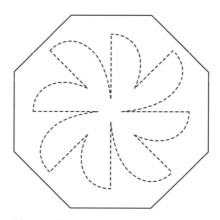

Diagram 60

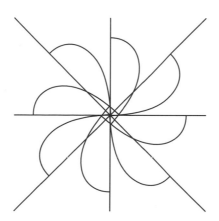

Diagram 61

DESIGN #21 features a cozy arrangement of overlapping teardrops with odd-shaped inner segments that float and rotate in space. The compact nature of this design makes it suitable for corner squares in latticework or in pieced blocks.

You probably have the perfect spot for **DESIGN #22**—a blend of angular and curved lines in a rotating format. Diagram 62 shows its basis—a combination of small and large teardrop templates with selective removal of lines.

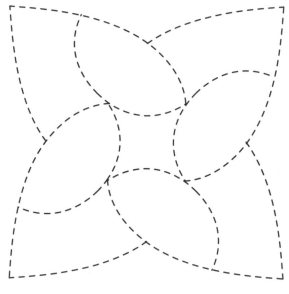

DESIGN #21

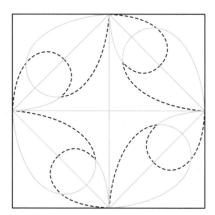

Diagram 62

Design #22 is a lean design, and you may want to add echo, stipple, or filler quilting lines in the inner and outer spaces. Continuous line quilters will be pleased to see that it also passes their test! (If you haven't already made a large teardrop template, see page 189.)

DESIGN #22

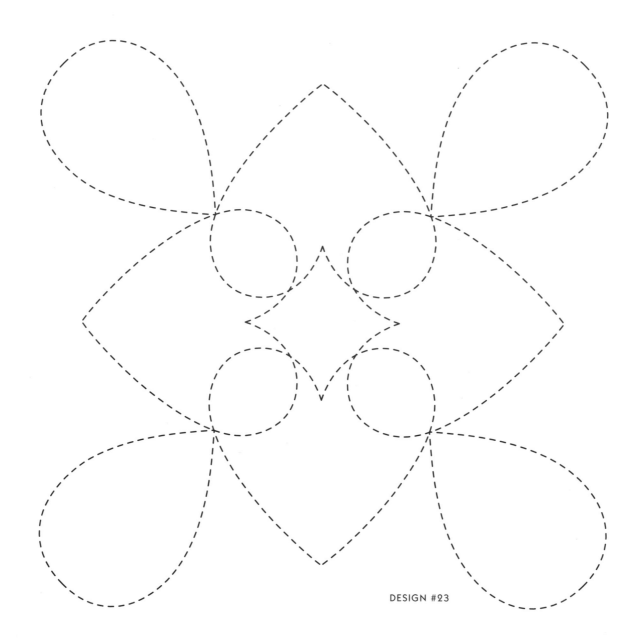

DESIGN #23

DESIGN #23 also features a com-bination of shapes—teardrops and hearts—in a symmetrical setting. It fills the space nicely and has the added feature of line continuity.

Floral shapes and flowing lines characterize **DESIGN #24.** What was conceived as a design for a triangular space has been multiplied to fit a block. Diagram 63 illustrates the

design basis on a triangle. The repeat in three other quadrants, with edges just touching, reveals the graceful lines and the secondary design—the inner cross.

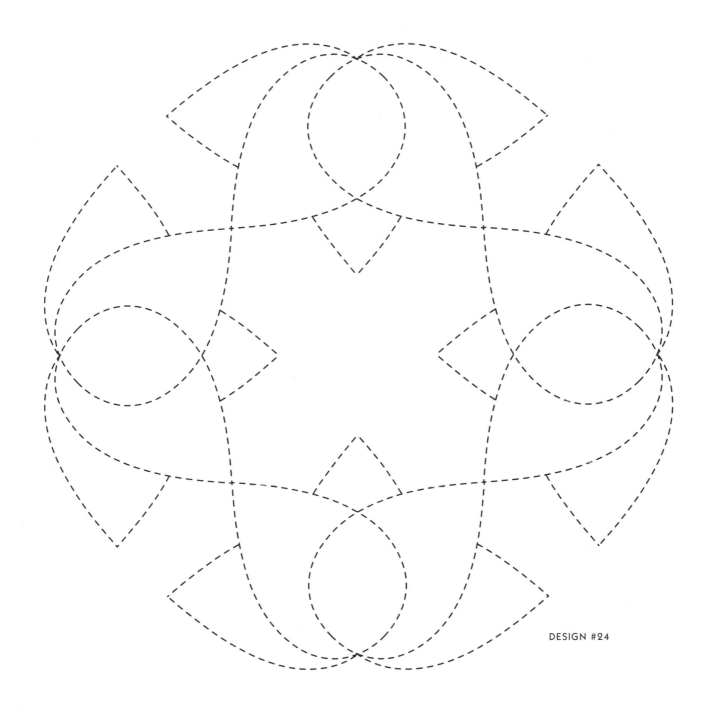

DESIGN #24

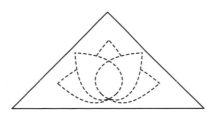

Diagram 63

DESIGN #25

DESIGN #25 utilizes both the small and large teardrops in a pattern that radiates from the center. The large outer sunburst is echoed by inner concentric designs.

Diagram 64

Diagram 64 shows the design basis and how selected lines have been removed. Although it is not fully continuous in nature, the quilting lines do grow and repeat in a sensible, stitchable fashion.

✦ *Now it's your turn!*

A 6-inch (15.2 cm) square has been prepared for you to try your own design on the **Workpage**. You may use any of the three templates. Or you may use them in combination, as in Design #23. Why not try using a partial template, as in Design #20? Play around with various positions on the square.

Here are some other ideas to try:

1. Get out your compass and draw a 6-inch (15.2 cm) circle and make a design to fit. Be sure to mark the center and divide it into workable sections.

2. Use your protractor and construct a hexagon or octagon (or enlarge Diagrams 59 and 60). Make a design to fit the space.

3. Make a simple small design, such as in Diagram 63. Then make three more like it and position them all together to discover your new, larger design.

If you favor working with smaller blocks of space, or if you're into miniatures, start with a smaller space such as a 3-inch (7.6 cm) square. Use the small teardrop in an overlapped format, or make a template of the tiny teardrop on page 189.

If you need designs for large blocks of space, make an appropriate size square, such as a 12-inch (30.5 cm) or 15-inch (38.1 cm) square. Divide the square into workable sections and use the larger version of the templates.

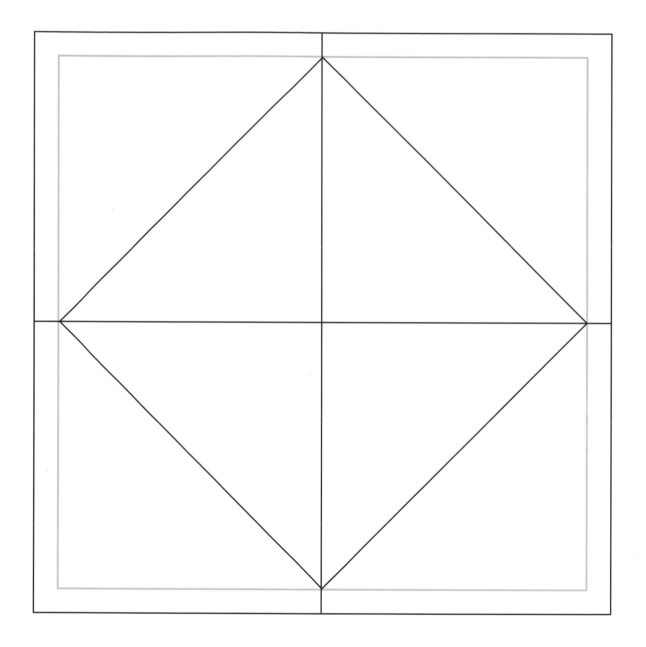

Triangles

OST QUILTING publications devote very little space to designs suitable for triangles. Following a futile search for patterns appropriate in style and size, quiltmakers often resort to the simple solution—chop a design for a square in half and tidy up the edges a bit. The result is usually a fragmented design, sometimes with literal loose ends. I've resorted to this process myself—starting with an attractive design for a block, slicing it in half for a side triangle, and cutting it once more for a corner triangle. The results were not always good.

The triangle designs in this book are designed specifically and intentionally for triangular spaces. They work on triangles. If they can be multiplied and also work in blocks and latticework, that is an added bonus. Many of them can, but it is not a guarantee. While the primary purpose of these designs is for use in the triangular places on your quilt, we can also consider multiplying them to fit a larger triangle or square. This is the reverse of what I described above (i.e. chopping a square design in half, and half again, to fit side and corner triangles). Many of these triangle designs can be used on a corner triangle, doubled (like a mirror image) for use on a side triangle, and quadrupled to fit a large square. Illustrations of this multiplicity of use are provided with selected designs.

TO MAKE DESIGNS #26–#31
DESIGN #26 is an unpretentious heart pattern for a small triangle. It combines gentle curves with cropped outer straight lines. The simplicity of the lines makes it suitable for doubling for a larger triangle, as shown in Diagram 65. Two designs have been placed adjacent to each other, and the common center line has been removed. If you imagine another full mirror image of Diagram 65, you will have a radiating heart design suitable for a square.

Diagram 65

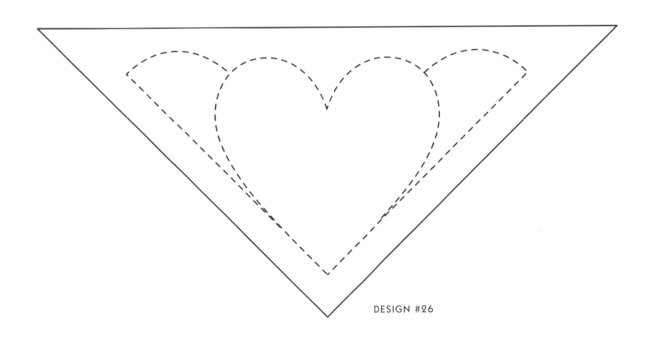

DESIGN #26

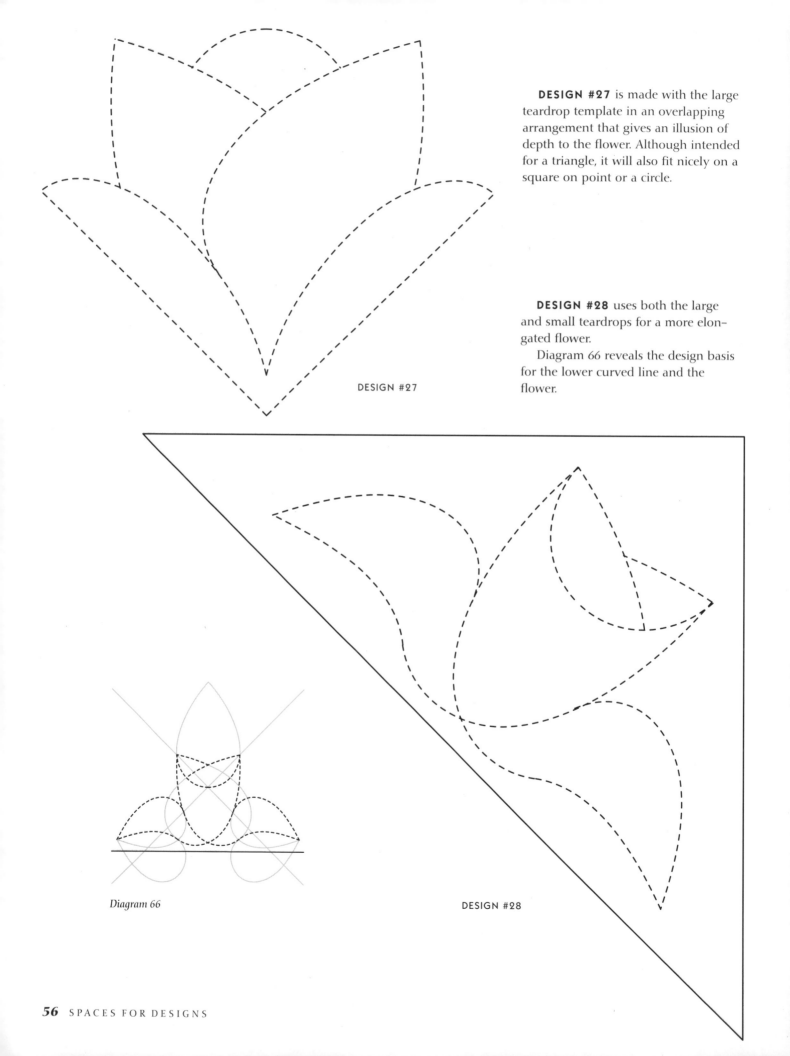

DESIGN #27 is made with the large teardrop template in an overlapping arrangement that gives an illusion of depth to the flower. Although intended for a triangle, it will also fit nicely on a square on point or a circle.

DESIGN #28 uses both the large and small teardrops for a more elongated flower.

Diagram 66 reveals the design basis for the lower curved line and the flower.

DESIGN #27

Diagram 66

DESIGN #28

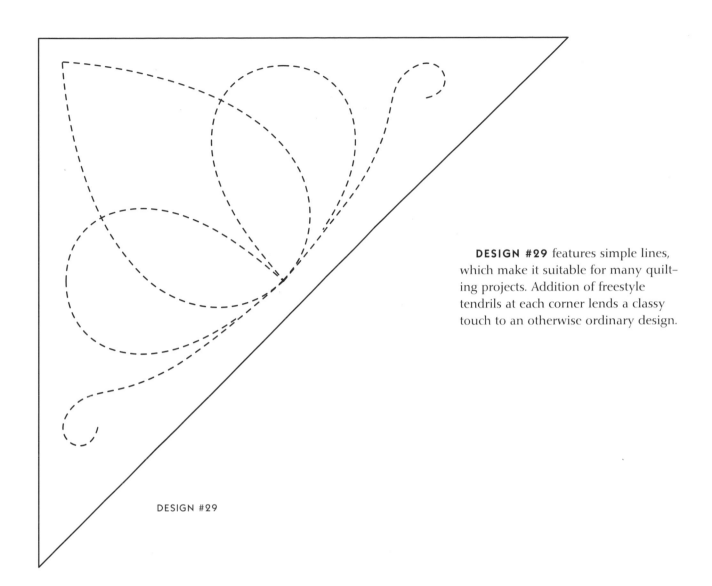

DESIGN #29 features simple lines, which make it suitable for many quilting projects. Addition of freestyle tendrils at each corner lends a classy touch to an otherwise ordinary design.

DESIGN #29

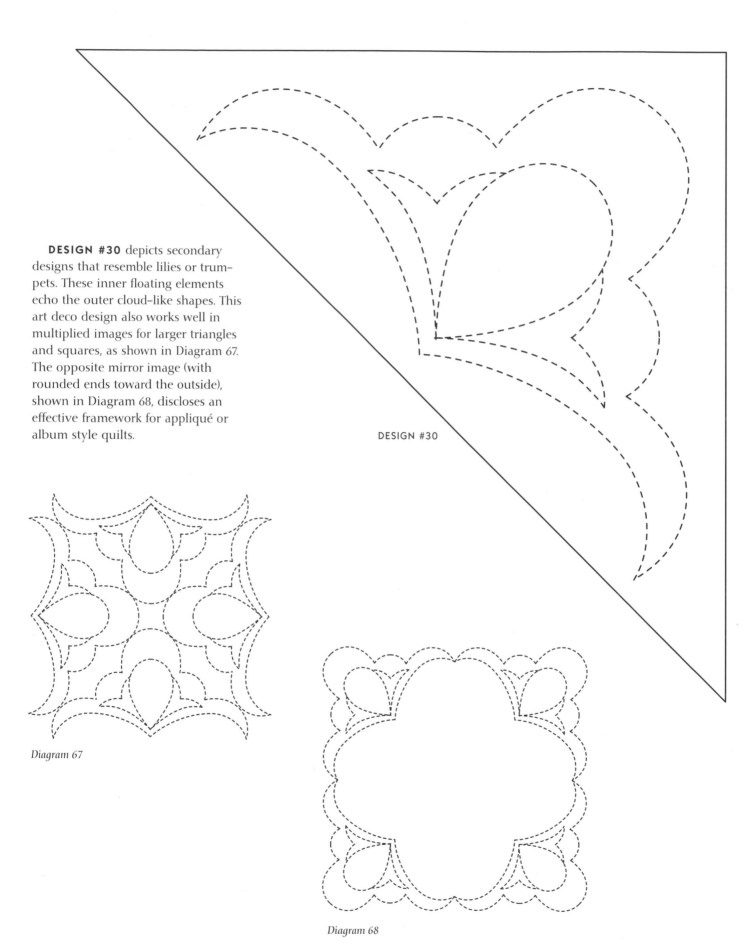

DESIGN #30 depicts secondary designs that resemble lilies or trumpets. These inner floating elements echo the outer cloud–like shapes. This art deco design also works well in multiplied images for larger triangles and squares, as shown in Diagram 67. The opposite mirror image (with rounded ends toward the outside), shown in Diagram 68, discloses an effective framework for appliqué or album style quilts.

DESIGN #30

Diagram 67

Diagram 68

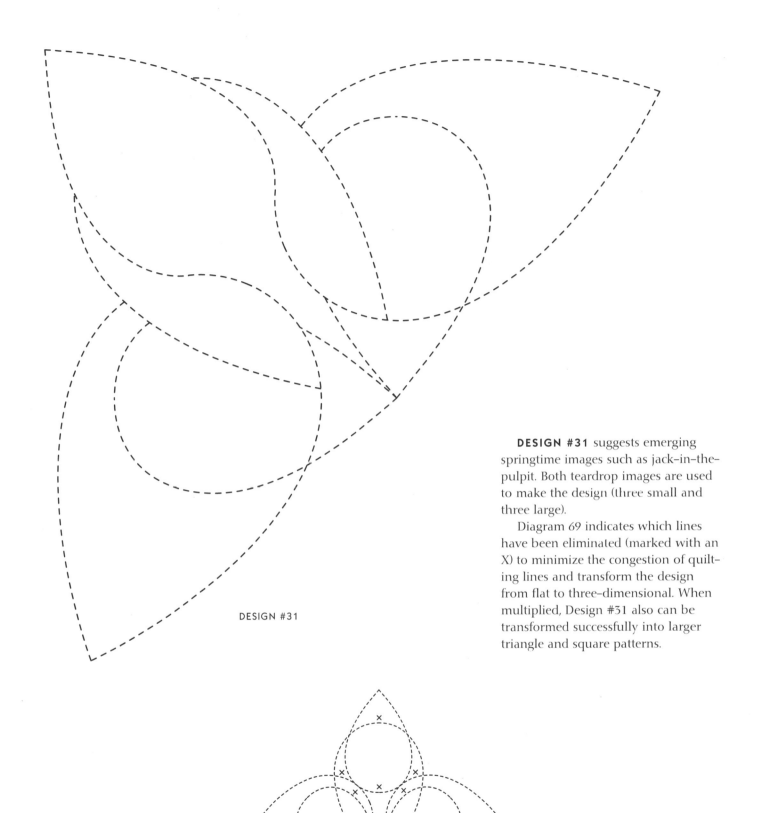

DESIGN #31 suggests emerging springtime images such as jack–in–the–pulpit. Both teardrop images are used to make the design (three small and three large).

Diagram 69 indicates which lines have been eliminated (marked with an X) to minimize the congestion of quilting lines and transform the design from flat to three-dimensional. When multiplied, Design #31 also can be transformed successfully into larger triangle and square patterns.

DESIGN #31

Diagram 69

Challenge

For an exciting exercise in design multiplicity, make four copies of Design #28. Place two designs flush with each other for a larger triangle format. Then try four designs with the flowers toward the center, their edges just touching, and see what you find. I think you'll be pleased.

Now it's your turn!

When attempting to create your own design for a triangular space, the first step is to measure the place on the quilt. Measure all sides of the area. Next, draw a triangle on paper exactly like the one on your quilt. Consider this your design area.

In order to avoid the placement of quilting lines on bulky seam areas, lightly pencil in 1/4 inch (.6 cm) clearance lines on all edges of the triangle. Examples are shown on the **Workpage.** Next, add some guidelines to divide the space into smaller workable sections. (Remember the key words–*pencil* and *lightly*). Now you are ready to take any template and create your own quilting design.

For your convenience, two triangle spaces, both prepared with clearance lines and guidelines, are provided on the following **Workpage.** Use these spaces to experiment with new triangular designs. But remember, when you plan a design specifically for the space on your quilt, make your paper triangle the same size as the one on the quilt. Good luck!

Rectangles

$\mathcal{P}$ERHAPS THIS IS the section for which you've been waiting. What to do in the latticework and borders? The eternal quilting question!

These border and latticework designs include all three shapes—the teardrop, the heart, and the flower. Some of the designs are given for the rectangle space only. Some have the added bonus of a corner treatment for the border.

In the workshop portion, some of the diagrams and designs will be reduced in order to fit the page. All designs, however, are eventually presented full-size, either in this section or on the foldout pattern insert at the back of the book.

TO MAKE DESIGN #32

We begin with overlapping teardrop images—a common motif for traditional quilting designs such as cables, plaiting, and other interwoven patterns. This design illustrates a cable–like pattern constructed from overlapping teardrop templates. It is suitable for a small rectangle or lattice. Selected lines have been removed; others have been highlighted.

This basic interwoven design can be multiplied and elongated for longer lattice pieces and borders, as illustrated in Diagram 70.

TO MAKE DESIGNS #33–#35

The next three designs are all based on the small teardrop, and are suitable for narrow sashings or borders. Each highlights different lines and shapes from the overlapping teardrop images. Design #33 features symmetrical interwoven patterns with secondary diamond shapes. Designs #34 and #35 are asymmetrical arrangements, one suggestive of twisted rope, the other more freestyle in line and motion.

The basis for these three designs is shown in Diagram 71. Perhaps you would like to try your hand at uncovering yet another quilting pattern for latticework and borders.

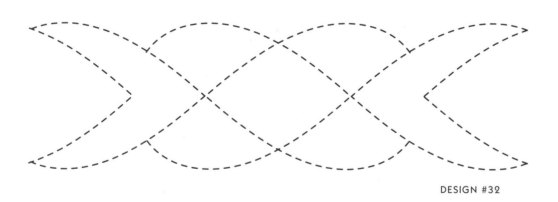

DESIGN #32

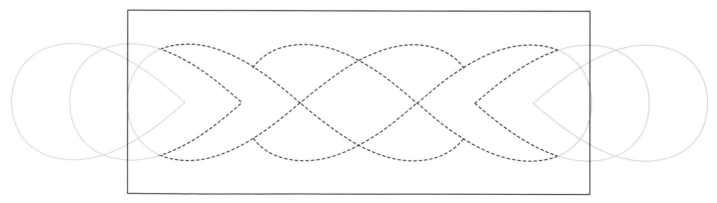

Diagram 70

Diagram 71

DESIGN #33

DESIGN #34

DESIGN #35

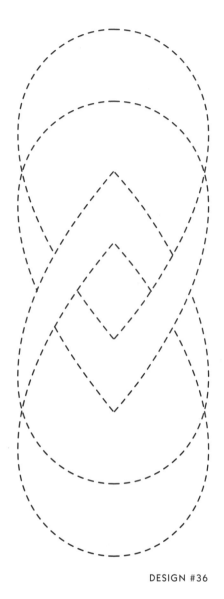

The next two designs show the interlocking nature of the teardrop template. This is an effective way to add a three–dimensional illusion to a quilting pattern. The concept of *Interlocking Designs* will be covered in depth in another section of this book. For now, we will concentrate only on two designs that are suitable for lattices or borders.

TO MAKE DESIGNS #36–#37

Four large teardrops comprise Design #36. Removal of selected lines creates an over–and–under effect of the images being chained together. Repetition of this design creates yet another interlocked pattern, as shown in Diagram 72. Additional segments can be added to accommodate longer lattices and borders. Check the pattern insert at the back of the book for Design #37.

DESIGN #36

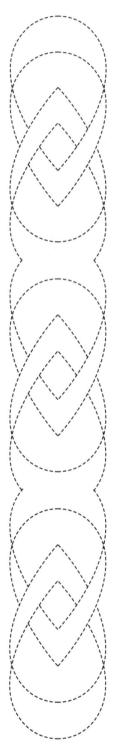

Diagram 72

THE REMAINING five designs are made to fit borders and corners. They can be used separately as borders only, or they can be applied to corners for a continuous design.

The first two designs use the teardrop templates, another uses the heart, and the last two are derived from the flower motif.

Because these five designs are larger than the pages of this book, they are included full size in the pattern section at the back of the book. Only the basic design elements are shown here.

TO MAKE DESIGNS #38–#42

Design #38 is a classic trailing vine utilizing the small teardrop. It is suitable for a border at least three inches (7.6 cm) wide. The addition of leaf vein lines and a continuous vine make the design more realistic. Refer to the oversize pattern sheet for a corner application of Design #38.

Design #39 brings the teardrop templates to life in the form of butterflies (or some similar flying creature). The butterflies can be used as an individual

pattern to fill a small rectangular space, or they can be combined to accommodate sashing and borders. Diagram 73 reveals the design basis–four small and two large teardrops. Refer to the oversize pattern sheet for the corner application of Design #39.

If you like this winged being, you can look forward to the formation of other unidentified flying objects in the section on *Design Extraction* later in the book.

Diagram 73

Design #40 is based on an overlapping heart template. In a single row, it resembles strings of street lights, and could be used on a narrow border. If the design is doubled and staggered, a secondary figure appears, as in Diagram 74. A full size border and corner rendition of Design #40 is on the foldout pattern insert.

Design #41 combines angular and flowing lines and can be stitched in a continuous line. The design basis is illustrated in Diagram 75. Think of it as two separate elements that run parallel to each other. A full–size corner rendition is included on the foldout pattern insert.

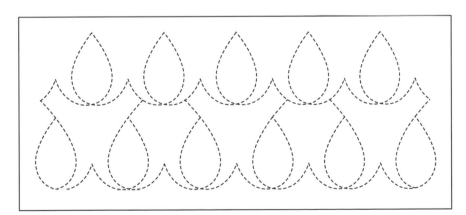

Diagram 74

Diagram 75

Design #42 is based on alternating flower images, as shown in Diagram 76. The newly formed miniature flower and ax head shapes combine in a carefree pattern suitable for borders or lattices. It can easily be extended to fit various border lengths. The basic design element (shown in Diagram 77) can be used as a stencil for marking the quilting design.

Refer to the back of the book for full size border and corner renditions of Designs #38, #39, #40, #41, and #42.

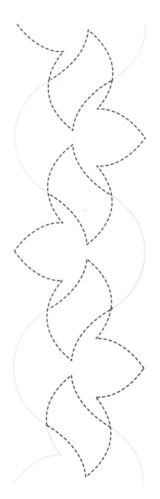

Diagram 76

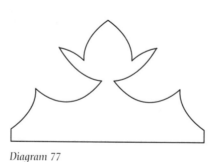

Diagram 77

 Now it's your turn!

The basic principles for designing a lattice or border are the same as for blocks and triangles. First define the space that is to be quilted. Measure it, and make a paper pattern the same size. Add the outer ¼ inch (.6 cm) clearance lines all around, pencil in guidelines to divide the space into smaller workable units, select a template, and proceed with your design.

A **Workpage** with two rectangular spaces is provided. Clearance lines and guidelines to divide the space are indicated. Select a template (teardrop, heart, or flower) and try your hand at border design.

Workpage

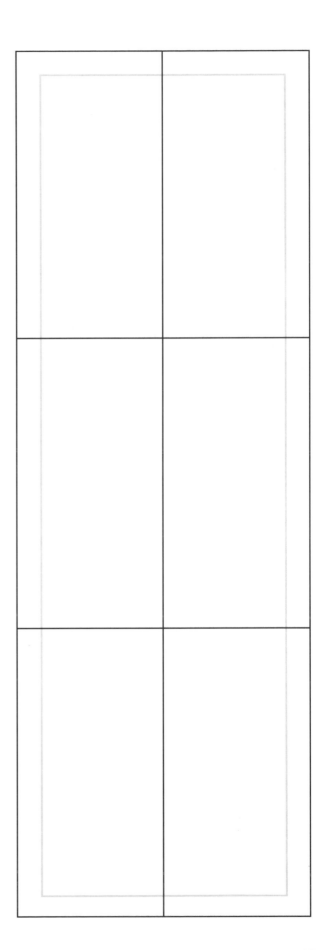

Special Techniques

UNLOCKING THE SECRETS OF QUILTING DESIGN

Positioning

OSITIONING refers to the placement of design elements. Quiltmakers are accustomed to seeing quilting designs placed in a radiating format from a central point, as was illustrated in the section on shapes. We have an inclination toward symmetrical designs. In this section we will explore other position options such as reversal of templates, proximity of images, and working from the outer edge of a space.

TO MAKE DESIGNS #43–#46

Designs #43 and #44 show the effect of reversal of templates. Both use four small teardrop images rotating around a central point. The main difference is that one points in and the other points out. The first one (#43) is angular at the center and rounded at the edges. The other (#44) is opposite, with its swirling spiral center and sharp outer edges.

Designs #45 and #46 illustrate the same reversal of templates as #43 and #44, but with positioning away from the center. They are more widely spaced and create a small diamond at the center.

All four designs are suitable for quilting. The positioning of the templates determines whether the design feels rounded or angular, snug or roomy.

Diagram 78 illustrates some possible placements of the small teardrop within the large teardrop. The differences are quite pronounced. Some are very smooth and balanced. Others reveal angular and asymmetrical images. An application of each of these four images is shown in Diagrams 79, 80, 81, and 82. These are not necessarily effective designs for quilting, but they do illustrate the varying effects of positioning.

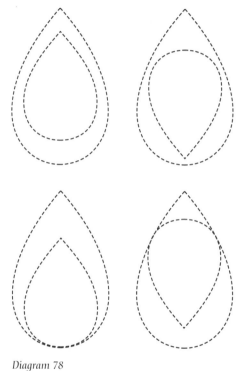

Diagram 78

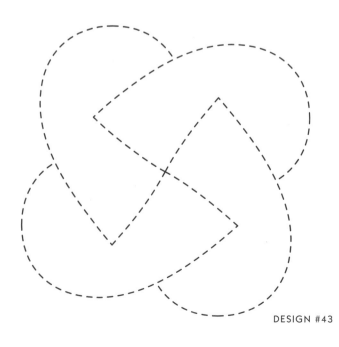

DESIGN #43

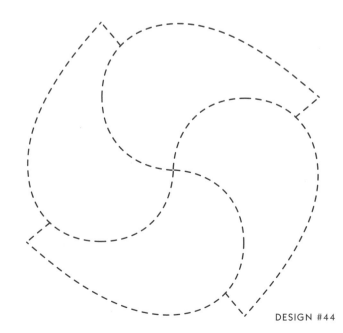

DESIGN #44

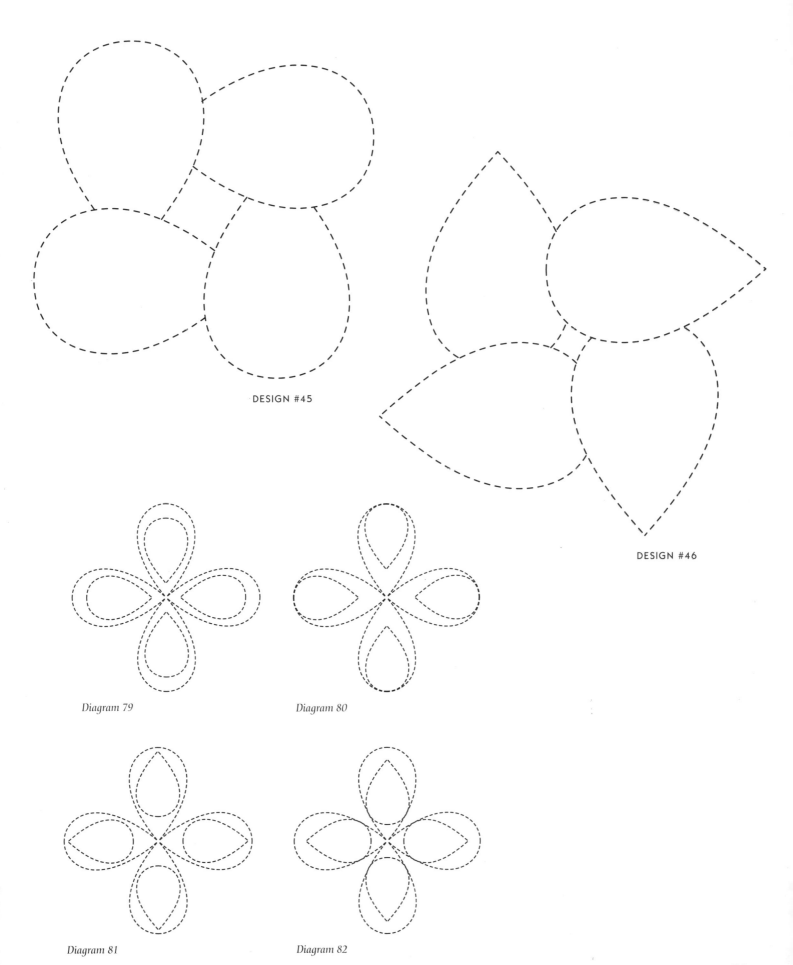

DESIGN #45

DESIGN #46

Diagram 79

Diagram 80

Diagram 81

Diagram 82

DESIGN #47 reveals a pattern more suitable for quilting. It utilizes one of the placement options from Diagram 78. Can you determine which one? Can you tell if this design can be quilted in one continuous line?

TO MAKE DESIGN #48

Positioning from the outer edge is illustrated in Design #48. To make this design, begin with a 6-inch (15.2 cm) square. Add the customary diagonal guidelines, and then add a second set of diagonal lines, as shown in Diagram 83. Place the point of the large teardrop at the center top, bottom, and sides, matching the line on the template with the diagonal line on the square. Lightly trace around the teardrop, as shown in Diagram 84.

Continue by marking locater dots where the outer edge of the teardrop intersects the diagonal line, as in Diagram 84.

Reposition the pointed end of the teardrop at the marked dot, and rotate the template until its side just touches the center top, bottom, and sides, as shown in Diagram 85. The template will be at a slight angle.

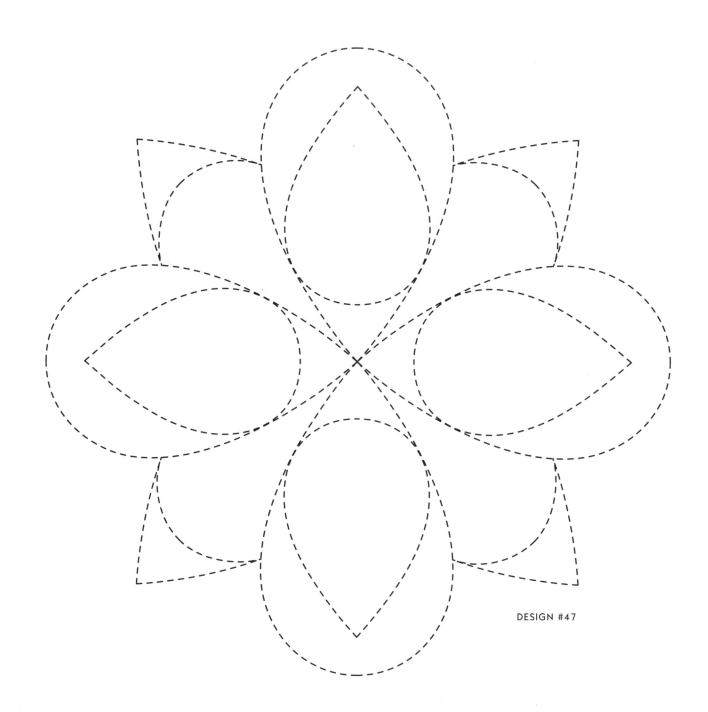

DESIGN #47

DESIGN #48

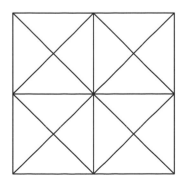

Diagram 83

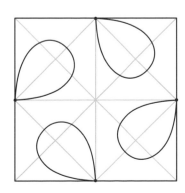

Diagram 84

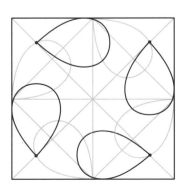

Diagram 85

DESIGN #49

TO MAKE DESIGN #49

The final positioning example combines placement from the outer edge with radiation from the center. Design #49 uses both the large and small teardrops. Begin with a 7$\frac{1}{2}$-inch (19 cm) square. Lightly mark the diagonal lines, as shown in Diagram 86. Place and trace the large teardrop template with the point at the center and the rounded ends toward the corners, as in Diagram 87.

Next, place the small teardrops at the outer edge, with the points at the center top, bottom, and sides. Match the line on the template with the diagonal guidelines on the square, as in Diagram 88. Highlight the completed Design #49 with broken lines.

 Now it's your turn!

This **Workpage** has a large square with outer edges and diagonal guidelines in place. Select whichever template you prefer, and experiment with placement. Try any place except the center! Perhaps you will want to make some extra copies of this **Workpage** so you can experiment with various placements and create your own quilting designs.

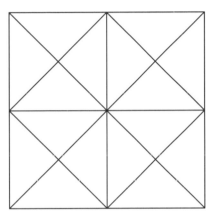

Diagram 86

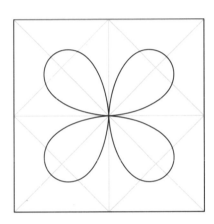

Diagram 87

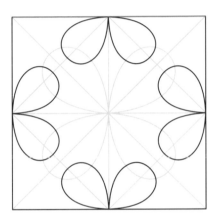

Diagram 88

Design Extraction

THIS IS NOT the place to begin reading this book. Save it for a day when you are totally uninspired and convinced that all the effective designs in the quilting world have already been discovered, published, and quilted.

When you return to this section, be prepared for an eye-opening exercise and the opportunity to quiz yourself on your ability to find hidden designs. Get ready to find unexpected designs in secret places.

The process of design extraction involves the removal of designs for separate consideration. To extract is to draw forth, or to pull out, using effort. The exercises in this section entail two steps: First, a thorough search of a pattern for hidden lines and shapes, and second, the highlighting of pinpointed designs. In short, we will search for and discover hidden designs.

Two examples are included. Both are based on the small teardrop, and

both are run-of-the-mill placements that radiate from the center. But they have some differences. Example A has half the teardrops pointed toward the center, and half toward the corners. Example B has all the teardrops pointed outward. Here's the other difference: Example A illustrates the design basis, extracts the designs, and highlights them. Example B illustrates the design basis and then you extract the designs and highlight them!

The preparation of Example A is given in Diagrams 89 and 90.

1. Begin with a 5-inch (12.7 cm) square of paper. Lightly mark the horizontal, vertical and diagonal guidelines.

2. Place the teardrop template with the point at the center and the rounded end toward the top. Trace around it, and repeat at the bottom and sides, as shown in Diagram 89.

3. Add the remaining images by placing the template with the rounded end at the center and the point toward the corner, as in Diagram 90.

I have selected twenty designs extracted from Example A. They illustrate the multiplicity of motifs that can be extracted from one pattern. I am not suggesting that all twenty are dynamic or even fully workable designs. Do not view them critically. Look at them without discrimination and consider their potential as latent designs, waiting to be molded into suitable patterns for quilting.

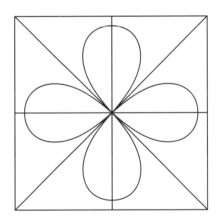

Diagram 89

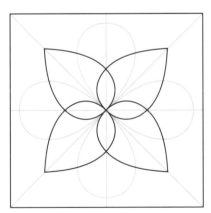

Diagram 90

EXAMPLE A

Now it's your turn!

The preparation of Example B is given in Diagrams 91 and 92.

1. Begin with a 5-inch (12.7 cm) square of paper and prepare it with guidelines, as in Diagram 91.

2. Place the teardrop template with the rounded end at the center and trace around it in the eight radiating positions, as in Diagram 92.

The **Workpage** (on page 91) includes two patterns of Example B for your use. Start looking for designs that can be extracted. You may highlight them on the **Workpage**, make copies of the **Workpage** for your personal use, or prepare your own squares according to the diagrams. You should be able to find numerous designs— maybe a dozen, or more.

Some of the possible designs

extracted from Example B are illus-trated in Appendix B at the end of the book. These are just some of the designs. Don't peek. Try the design extraction process first. Test yourself on your ability to see beyond the original teardrop template into the realm of potential designs. Most important, keep in mind there are many possible answers, but there are no wrong answers!

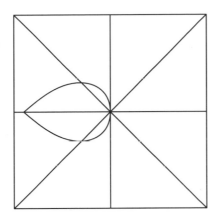

Diagram 91

Diagram 92

EXAMPLE B

Secondary Designs

E'VE ALREADY mentioned secondary designs in earlier portions of this book. Now let's discuss and illustrate them in more detail.

Secondary designs are easier to describe and illustrate than to define. They are the unexpected designs, often the background or negative space of a given area. They are the fresh shapes that may seem entirely unrelated to the primary design. Secondary designs may bear little resemblance to the original motif. They are usually a welcome surprise.

Several examples of secondary designs are shown in this section. The basis for each design is given, so you can understand its derivation.

TO MAKE DESIGNS #50–#53

Design #50 resembles the familiar Maltese Cross. It is formed by the placement of four teardrop templates. When straight lines are added to link the truncated teardrops, this secondary design comes into focus. The teardrop is no longer dominant. It has been replaced by the cross, as shown in Diagram 93.

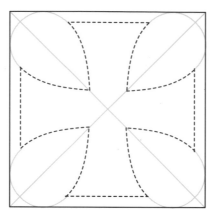

Diagram 93

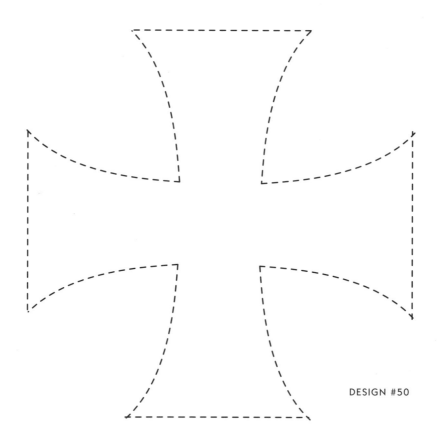

DESIGN #50

Design #51 produces a related secondary design when the four teardrops are reversed. Diagram 94 illustrates the placement of templates and straight lines that result in this anvil–like design.

Design #52 yields a slightly more active secondary design when the four teardrops are angled at each corner, as in Diagram 95. This asymmetrical placement adds a sense of motion to Design #52. A similar design can be made with the large teardrop.

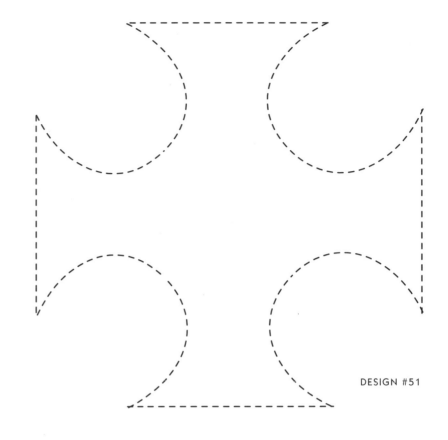

DESIGN #51

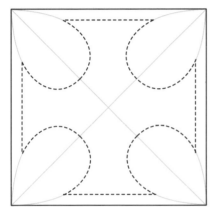

Diagram 94

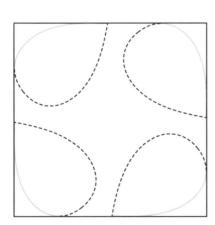

Diagram 95

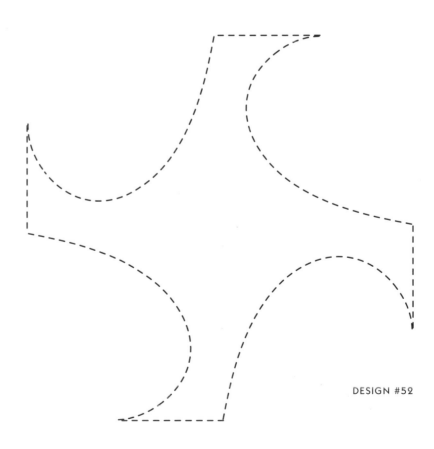

DESIGN #52

DESIGN #53

Design #53 is slightly more complex. It, too, is based on the small
teardrop.

Diagram 96 shows the positioning
of templates for the secondary designs
that branch out from the center.

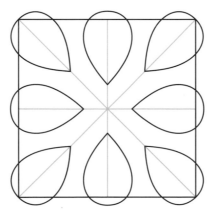

Diagram 96

TO MAKE DESIGN #54

Design #54 takes a different direction. Teardrops are placed in overlapping pairs in each corner, as shown in Diagram 97. The whimsical secondary star at the center may be a little bent out of shape, but surely worthy of space on somebody's quilt. A more elaborate rendition of Design #54 is included in the **Portfolio** section.

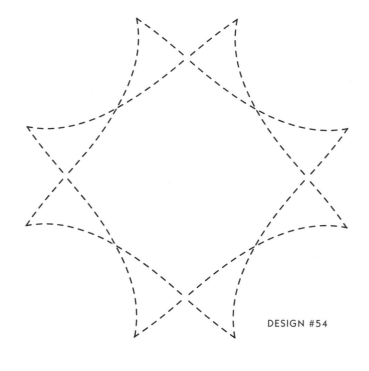

DESIGN #54

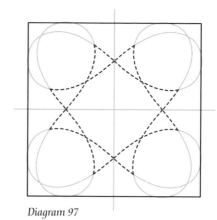

Diagram 97

TO MAKE DESIGNS #55 AND #56

The next design rotates from the center. Design #55 uses both small and large teardrop templates. The overlapping shapes create the pinwheel style pattern, as shown in Diagram 98.

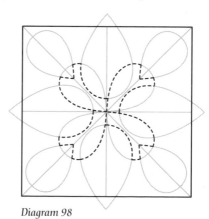

Diagram 98

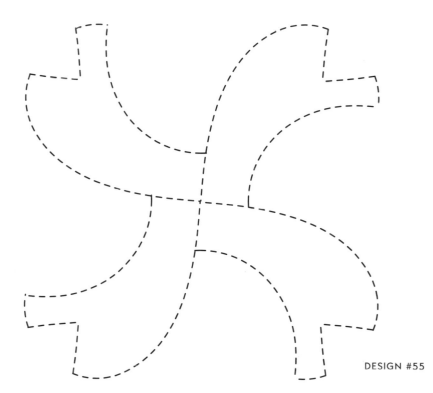

DESIGN #55

The final secondary design can be isolated and used by itself or as the complete Design #56. The basis is the overlapping arrangement of small teardrops shown in Diagram 99. Some inner lines have been removed to reveal the inner secondary design. Continuous line quilters can add this design to their portfolios.

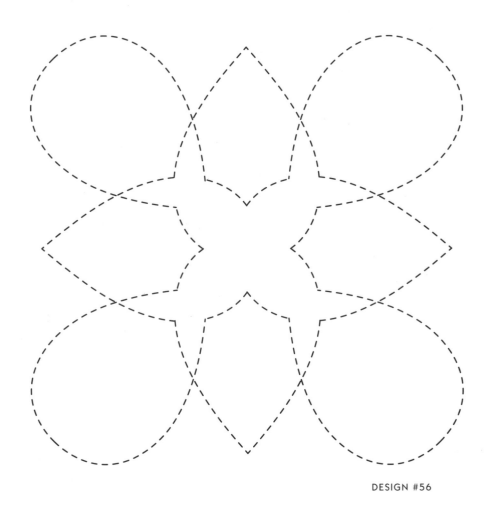

DESIGN #56

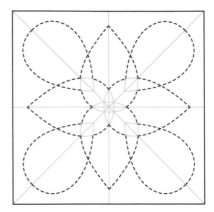

Diagram 99

✦ *Now it's your turn!*

There are no specific instructions on how to create your own secondary designs. Sometimes they just happen. It is less a matter of telling or even showing you how to make them as it is a matter of being on the lookout for them.

Keep your eyes wide open, and don't focus on the template that is being used. Instead, pay attention to what is going on between the templates as you trace them. Inspect the background and negative space for intriguing designs.

Also pay attention to the new shapes that form when templates overlap one another. Highlight anything that is fresh and appealing.

A **Workpage** is ready for you. Choose a template (try a new shape if you haven't tried all three yet) and begin your design. Watch for the unexpected in the unplanned spaces.

Adding Motion

MANY QUILTING PATTERNS can be improved by the addition of motion. The feeling of activity usually adds interest to a design. The concept of motion in quilt patterns is sometimes described as active versus passive, one implying more energy, the other more acquiescence.

The examples in this section illustrate how stationary designs can be converted to active designs. The process is not difficult; it mostly involves the use of an eraser or a bottle of white correction fluid.

The design in Diagram 100 can be described as passive. It is totally symmetrical. Removal of just a few short line segments can propel the design into motion. When the line segments marked with an X are removed, the design is transformed from passive to active. **DESIGN #57**, a spinning four-pointed star, is the result.

A more complex example is shown in Diagram 101. (Does this design seem familiar? It is yet another derivative from the Example B exercise in the section on *Design Extraction*.) This concentric flower pattern is an effective quilting design as is. However, it can readily be converted into activity. Diagram 102 indicates which lines could be eliminated. The completed **DESIGN #58** (on the next page) has the best of both worlds—a fixed center star and a rotating outer star.

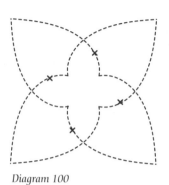

Diagram 100

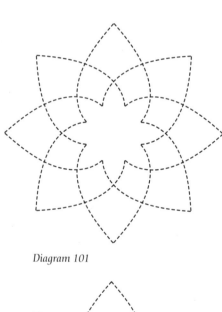

Diagram 101

Diagram 102

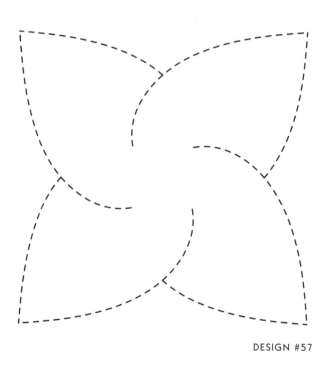

DESIGN #57

Diagram 103 reveals a symmetrical design quite suitable for quilting. However, it cannot be described as energetic. It also suffers from congestion (too many quilting lines meeting at certain points). Removal of selected inner line segments (indicated in Diagram 104) will remedy both situations. **DESIGN #59** has a center that has come alive, and the number of intersecting lines has been reduced. Can you think of other ways to modify this design for increased activity?

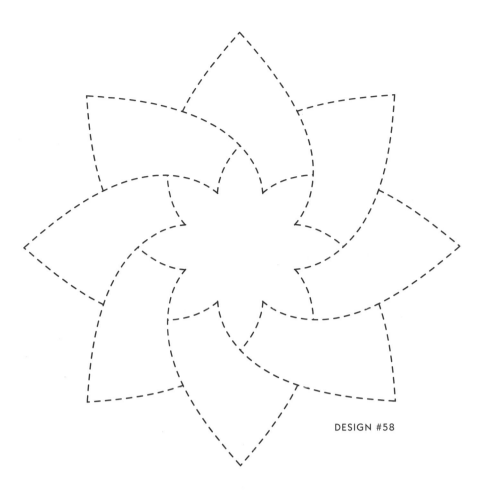

DESIGN #58

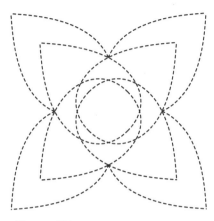

Diagram 103

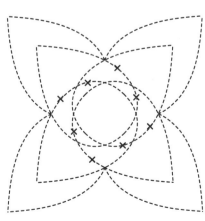

Diagram 104

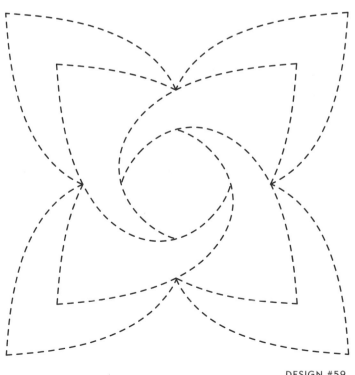

DESIGN #59

Diagram 105 features overlapping large teardrops in a symmetrical format. Removal of just four short line segments (marked with an X) will propel the design into motion. Suddenly an otherwise passive pattern is transformed into a pair of four-legged figures rotating in opposite directions, as in **DESIGN #60.**

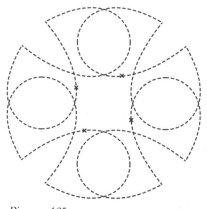

Diagram 105

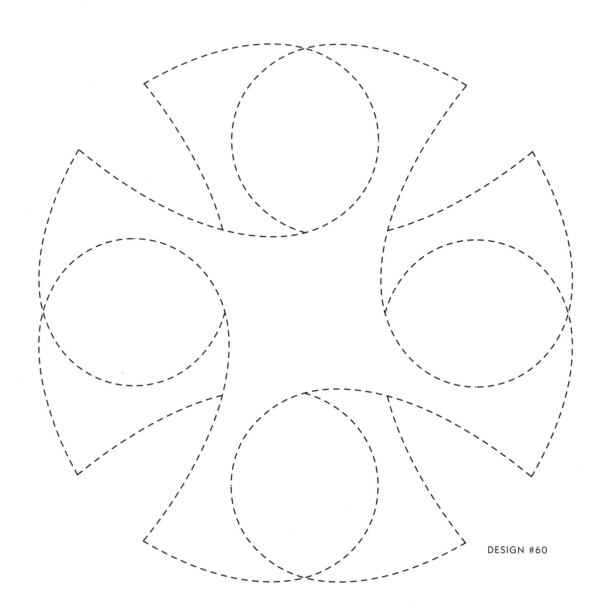

Now it's your turn!

The **Workpage** has two opportunities for you. Use the squares to make your own stationary design. Then select and remove line segments to convert it to a design with motion.

The other exercise involves **DESIGN #61**, which is a basic overlapping heart design. Examine it and indicate which lines might be removed to convert it to a rotating pattern. Some solutions can be found in **Appendix C.** (Don't peek before you try!)

DESIGN #60

Workpage

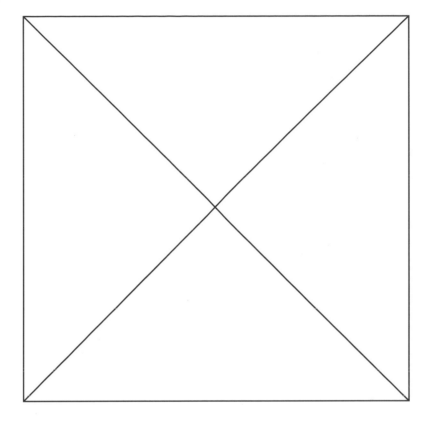

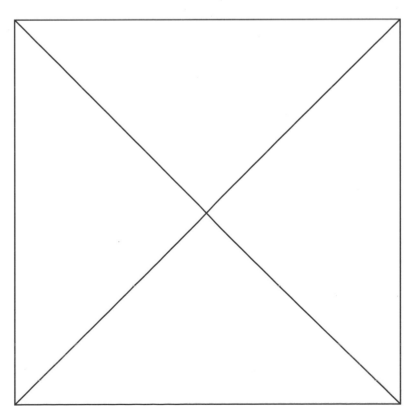

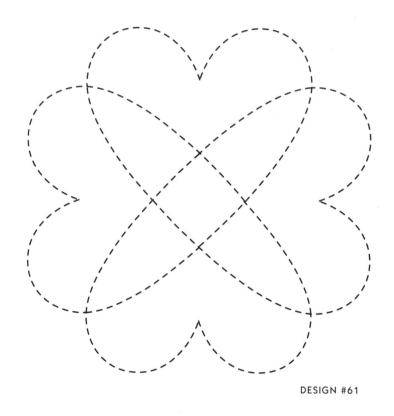

DESIGN #61

Interlocking Designs

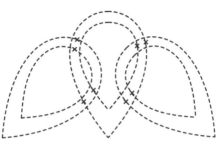

THIS SECTION could be called "Adding the Third Dimension to Your Designs." The phenomenon of inter-locking changes designs from two–dimensional to three–dimensional. The outcome is more depth and realism. Interlocking designs give the sensation that you could literally reach into them or reach through them, into the space on the other side.

I have found it pays to have your wits about you when working with interlocking designs. More often than not, I find myself highlighting and crossing over and under in the wrong places. Especially in this section, the eraser is an essential tool!

Some interlocking designs suitable for lattices and borders are included in the section on rectangles (Designs #36 and #37). The examples here include designs appropriate for squares, tri-angles, and borders.

DESIGN #62 utilizes the small and large teardrops in a chained arrange-ment. This is accomplished by an over and under linking of the three ele-ments. Diagram 106 indicates which lines have been removed.

A more intriguing design results when the small teardrops are reversed, as in **DESIGN #63**. The shapes are more angular, the lines less smooth than the previous example.

Another option is used in **DESIGN #64.** The small and large teardrops are placed with rounded ends flush with each other.

Diagram 106

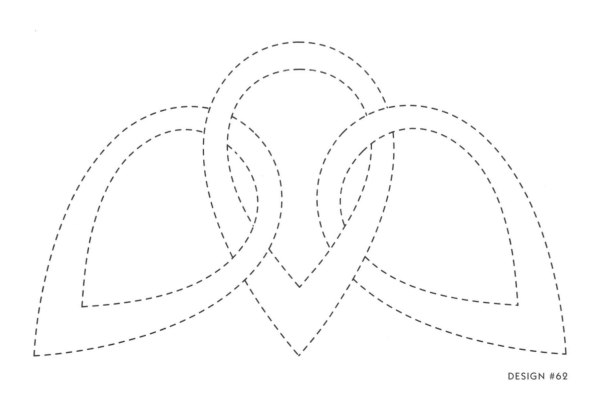

DESIGN #62

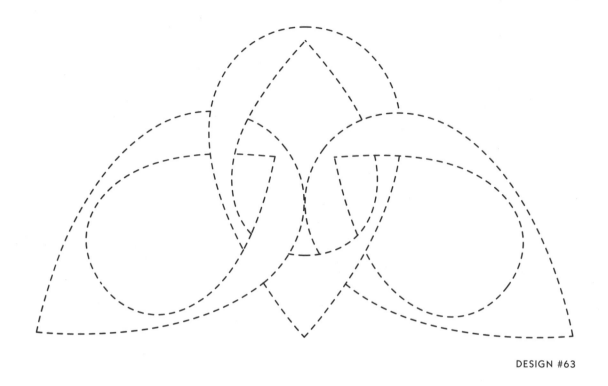

DESIGN #63

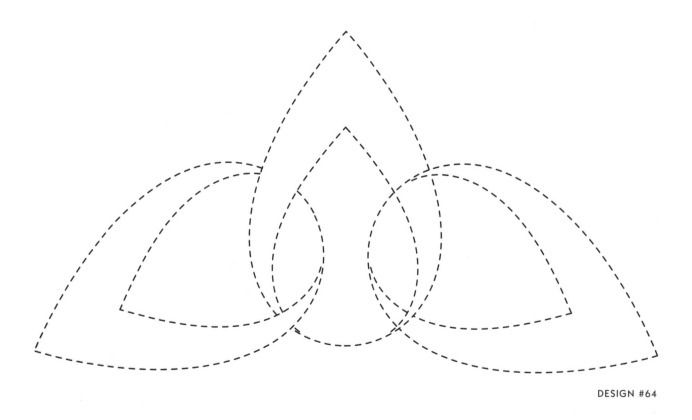

DESIGN #64

DESIGN #65 is suitable for a lattice about 3 by 9 inches (7.6 by 22.9 cm). It is fully interlocking, but more importantly, fully expandable on either end. It is adaptable for lattices and borders of any length. Simply reverse the teardrops and add units at either end.

The next two designs are appropriate for squares 7½ inches (19 cm) or larger. **DESIGN #66** is as lively as any in the book. One template (the large teardrop) has been positioned from the outside of the block in an asymmetrical format. In addition to its interlocking quality, it also creates a secondary design, the four-pronged figure at the center.

The heart templates in **DESIGN #67** have been modified slightly to create an interlocking effect. Once again, the orderly arrangement of over and under suggests the third dimension. An inner circle locks the tips of the hearts and creates the secondary cross design. This design is appropriate set either on point or on edge.

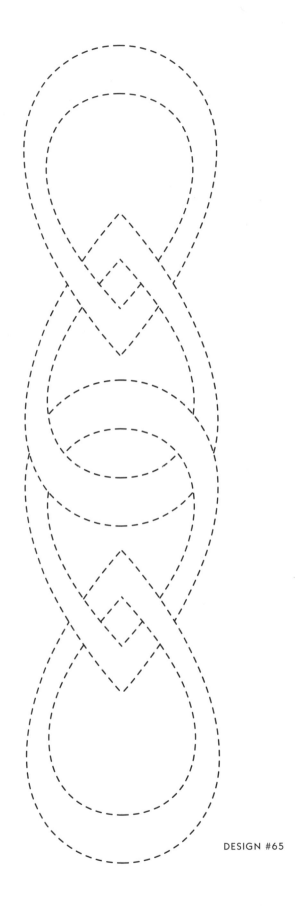

DESIGN #65

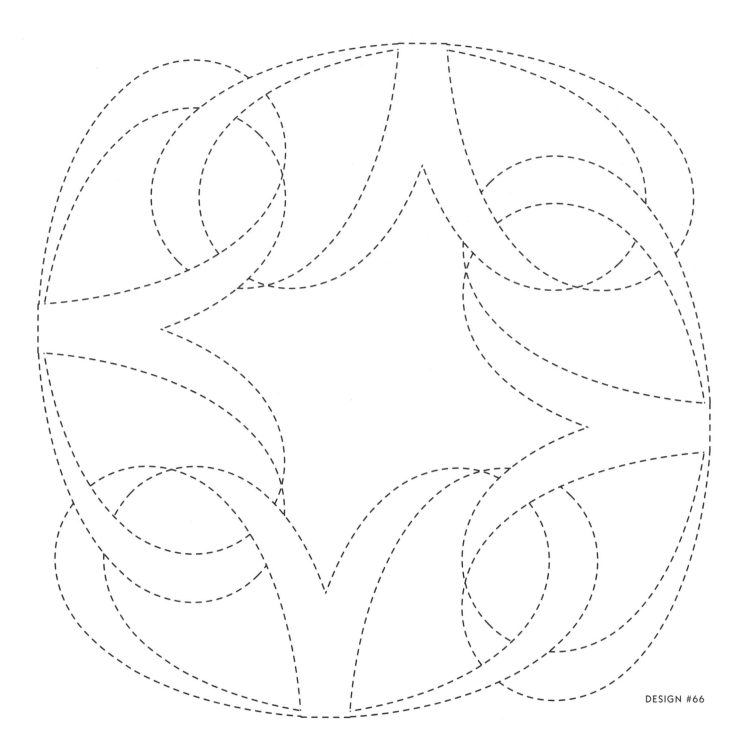

DESIGN #66

DESIGN #67

❋ *Now it's your turn!*

Perhaps the easiest way to make your interlocking design is to begin with paired templates, such as the small and large teardrops or two of the hearts.

A rectangular space has been provided on the **Workpage.** Use the small and large teardrops, one placed inside the other, and see if you can make them interlock.

Use two of the heart templates from page 190 on the **Workpage** square. Position and super-impose one over the other until an interwoven element appears. Then highlight and expand on the design.

Your designs need not be fully interlocking. If they only give the suggestion of being interlocked, you have acquired this special technique.

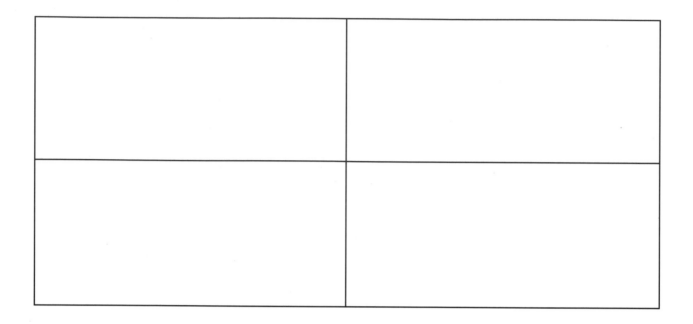

Continuous Line Designs

THE PHENOMENON of continuous line quilting designs has acquired a place of prominence in recent years. With the popularity and proliferation of machine quilting, more and more quiltmakers are searching for designs that can be stitched non-stop.

Continuous line designs are those in which the entire pattern can be stitched with only one start and one stop. The line of stitching is unbroken. It may cross over itself, or duplicate itself momentarily, but it remains unbroken. The real advantage to reducing the number of starts and stops is that the tedium of dealing with thread ends, knots, and unsightly backstitches and lockstitches is eliminated.

The preference for continuous line designs is not limited to machine quilters. Hand quilters also take advantage of uninterrupted lines to reduce the number of starts and stops, and to avoid frequent passing through of the needle.

Many of the designs in this book are continuous line. They are scattered throughout the **Workshop** and **Portfolio** sections, sometimes presented to illustrate another design technique.

Oftentimes, continuous line designs just happen by themselves, not intentionally.

After you finish this section, go back and page through the book again, looking more closely at the designs to see which ones may also be continuous. When you locate one, put your finger at an intersection and trace along the stitching lines to see if you can cover the entire design without lifting your finger. If you succeed, the design probably qualifies as continuous. Some continuous line designs are easy to detect. Others are less obvious, and some are downright deceptive! As you study the designs in this section and learn to make your own, you will also become more adept at analyzing other patterns for line continuity.

The six designs included here range from simple to complex. All can be stitched in one unbroken line, beginning and ending at the same point. I have indicated a possible starting and ending point on each design with a small dot. In most cases, there are many possible starting points. You may find one that is more suitable to your method or style of quilting. Study each example to find the other starting point possibilities.

Directional arrows and numbered line segments for stitching are included on the first three examples. As with starting points, there are usually several options for stitching direction and order. Quiltmakers typically have a personal preference for direction and order of continuous line stitching. In the final three examples, I leave that choice up to you. Examine them to determine what you think is the logical direction and order for stitching.

DESIGN #68 can easily be stitched in one stroke by beginning at the dot and working in a counter-clockwise fashion around the pattern. The order of stitching is indicated by the num–

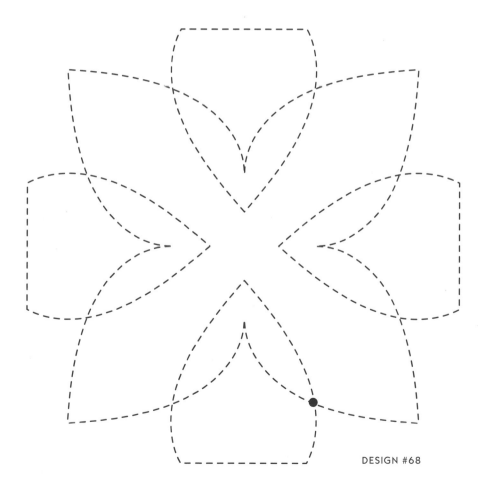

DESIGN #68

bered line segments (1 through 8) in Diagram 107. After the 8th line segment (which is in the same position as the 1st line segment), simply repeat the stitching order in the other sections of the design. You will finish where you began, on the line segment marked "end".

Put your finger on the starting point on Design #68 and see if you can trace over the entire pattern without lifting your finger. Eventually you will feel a natural rhythm in the flow and repetition of the pattern.

DESIGN #69 is a fundamental design based on overlapping large teardrops. A starting point is indicated. What other places would make suitable starting and ending points? In which direction should you go? In what order? Diagrams 108 and 109 illustrate two good options. Trace your finger along the arrows to feel the orderliness and continuity.

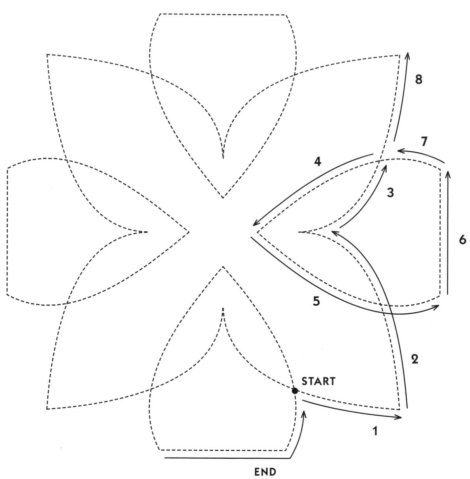

Diagram 107

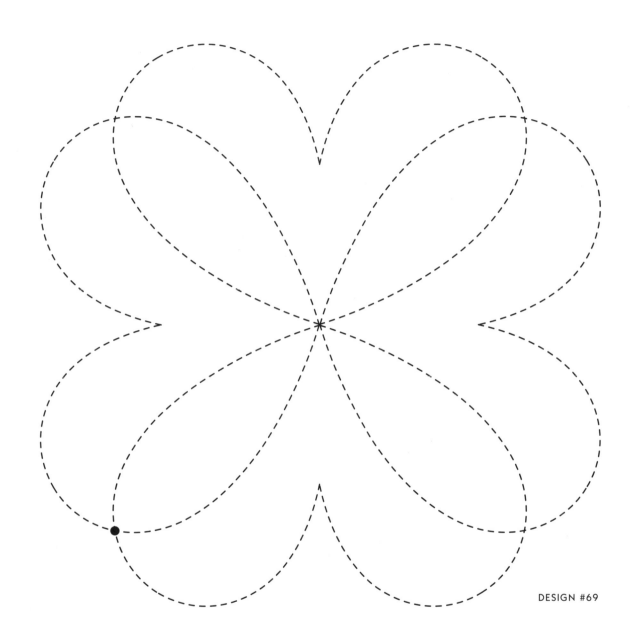

DESIGN #69

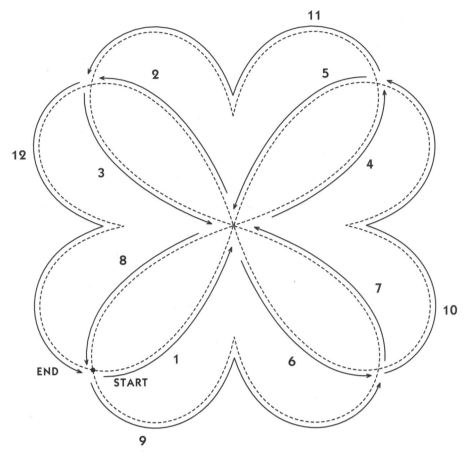

Diagram 108

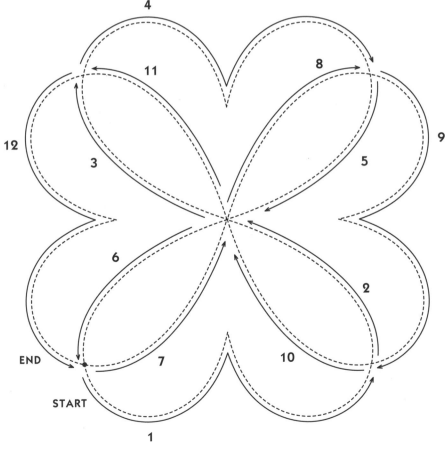

Diagram 109

DESIGN #70

The graceful lines of **DESIGN #70** make it seem like a natural candidate for continuous line quilting. In addition to fluid lines, it also has an inner secondary design (whales' tails?) that could be isolated and quilted on a small square.

A starting point for continuous line stitching is indicated. Can you determine the logical direction and order? **Clue:** Think of the design as two separate large designs, as illustrated in Diagrams 110 and 111. Then imagine them superimposed one over the other. Select any point where the two designs intersect and plan your stitching accordingly. Diagram 112 shows a workable plan.

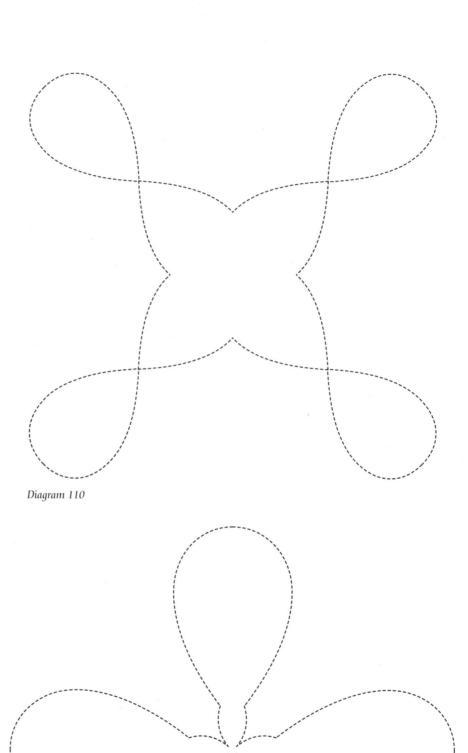

Diagram 110

Diagram 111

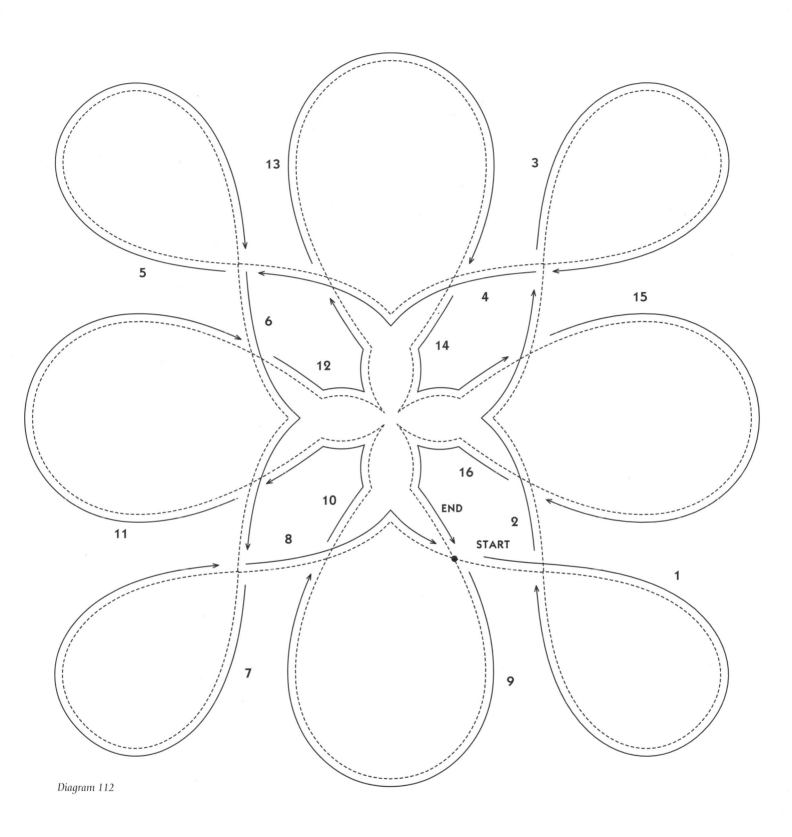

Diagram 112

Now it's your turn!

The remaining examples, **DESIGNS #71, #72,** and **#73,** are slightly more intricate. Examine each to find possible starting (and ending) points. Then consider a sensible direction and order for stitching. Determine a plan that will work well for you. There are several good options, some of which are shown in **Appendix C.** But don't look there until you have tried it here!

 Challenge

Numerous continuous line designs are scattered throughout the book. For additional practice at determining line continuity, refer back to these selected designs: #13, #23, #47, #49, #54, #56, and #61. Study them, and then indicate the starting point, a direction for stitching, and an order of stitching for each design. Good luck!

DESIGN #71

DESIGN #72

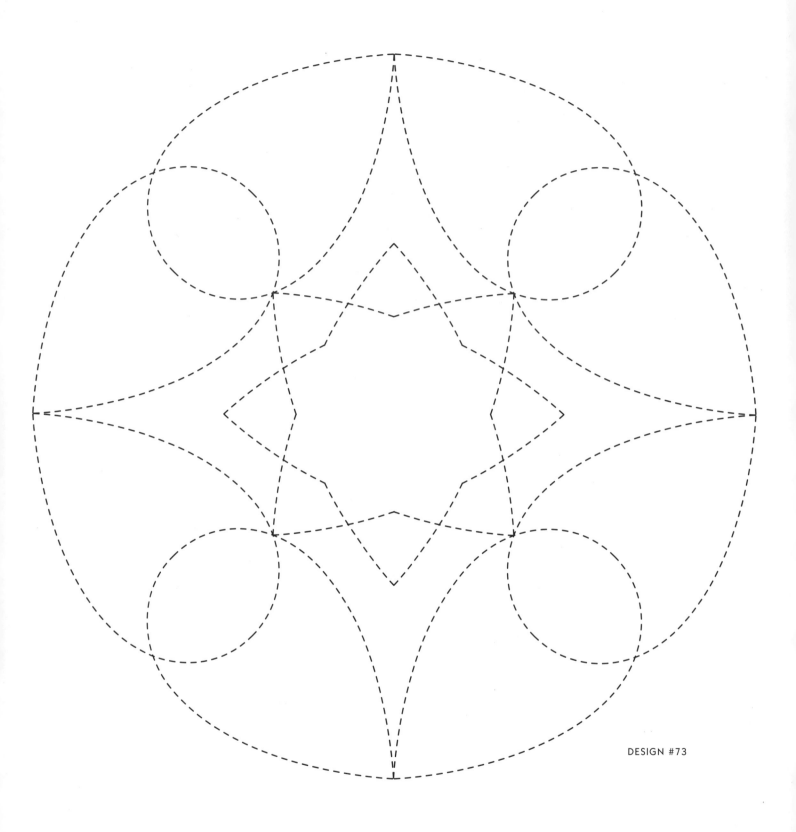

DESIGN #73

Transferring Designs

Q UILTMAKERS are frequently puzzled about how to get their newly created quilting designs onto the fabric. There seems to be a sense of mystery about the transfer of design to stencil to fabric. Many quilt-makers suddenly appear helpless.

Some designers have attempted to make true stencils, that is, plastic or paper perforated with the design. The results are not always satisfactory. Perhaps you have tried making your own stencils using a cutting board and a sharp knife. It is a challenging task, at best. At worst, the results can be disas-trous—uneven slits and slots and falling-apart pieces of plastic, and pos-sible nicks and cuts on your fingers.

However, there is no need to remain paralyzed about transferring your design onto the fabric. Many designs can be made without making a stencil full of holes. Often what we need is just another way of looking at the design.

In this final section of **Special Techniques,** I illustrate another way of making quilt stencils. I refer to this method as *multiple marking templates.* It simplifies the design transfer process, and it works for many designs.

The process is essentially one of learning to see the stencil in a different way. After you study several examples, you will have the chance to test your own vision!

TO MAKE TEMPLATES FOR DESIGN #74

Study the design. A traditional plas-tic stencil with narrow slots would be convenient, but it would be time-con-suming and challenging to construct. A sensible alternative is to use *multiple marking templates.* Study the design and

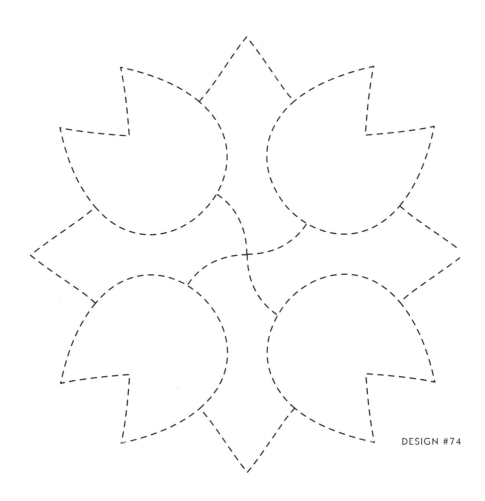

DESIGN #74

try to separately envision the outer shape, some inner shapes, or some smaller units within the design.

A good place to begin is with the outer shape. An intact template (from plastic or other suitable template material) of the outer shape, as shown in Diagram 113, includes the majority of lines in the design. The curved lines that remain in the center can be included in a second template, as shown in Diagram 114. Together, these two templates will provide all the quilting lines necessary for Design #74.

To mark the design on fabric, begin with the large template (Diagram 113) and mark the outer edge of the pattern. Then place the small template (Diagram 114) over the marked outer design, being careful to match the outer points, as in Diagram 114. Mark the inner curved lines. Then reposition (rotate) the small template to complete the inner lines in the remainder of the design, as in Diagram 115. Re-position the small template to complete the final stem line.

The use of these two fairly easy-to-make templates is a much simpler task than making a traditional stencil with intermittent, narrow slots.

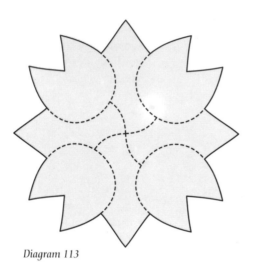

Diagram 113

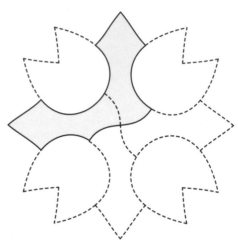

Diagram 114

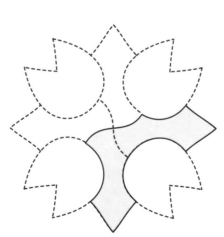

Diagram 115

DESIGN #75

TO MAKE TEMPLATES FOR DESIGN #75

A similar procedure can be used for Design #75. First consider only the outer shape, which would cover all the solid lines in Diagram 116. This is the first template. Then look for an inner shape that includes most of the inner lines. The template in Diagram 117 includes half of the inner lines. When the template is properly superimposed over the first template, with matched outer points, some of the inner lines can be drawn in. When the template is rotated 45 degrees, the remaining lines can be marked to complete the design.

Both of the templates for Design #75 are easy to make and easy to mark—much easier than cutting a traditional plastic stencil.

Diagram 116

Diagram 117

DESIGN #76

TO MAKE TEMPLATES FOR DESIGNS #76 AND #77

Design #76 can also be transferred with two basic templates. Begin with a pattern of the outer edge, as in Diagram 118. Next, make a second small template of the inner flower, as in Diagram 119. Reposition the second template to mark the remaining inner floral designs.

Diagram 118

Diagram 119

Now it should be easier for you to see the outer and inner shapes that are potential templates for marking designs. Look at Design #77. The first logical template is the outer edge, as shown in Diagram 120. The inner eight–pointed figure in Diagram 121 completes the lines in the design. First mark the outer edges. Then position the inner template over it to complete the design.

Diagram 120

Diagram 121

DESIGN #77

An alternative solution to Design #77 is to make a small template of only a portion of the inner shape, as shown in Diagram 122. Place it over the outer design, and rotate it to complete the four sections. A savings in time and template materials is the advantage to this alternative method.

Diagram 122

Not all quilting designs conform so well to this *multiple marking templates* method. But when it can be done this way, the benefits are clear. A good portion of the time–consuming and nerve–wracking part of stencil–making is eliminated.

✳ *Now it's your turn!*

The final two Designs, #78 and #79, are for your perusal. Study them to find a logical *multiple marking template* method for each of them. Each can be done with two templates. The **Workpages** include space for you to indicate your suggestions for templates.

Begin by considering the outer shape. Then determine which lines remain in the inside. Plan a second template to include some or all of these lines. The second template may require repositioning.

Suggestions for *multiple marking templates* for Designs #78 and #79 are given in **Appendix C** in the back of the book. Compare them with your choices. You may have a better solution.

Once you have mastered the concept of *multiple marking templates,* you will discover and create many designs that can be marked in this manner. As you page through the **Portfolio** section of this book, watch for designs that would be good candidates for *multiple marking templates.*

DESIGN #78

DESIGN #79

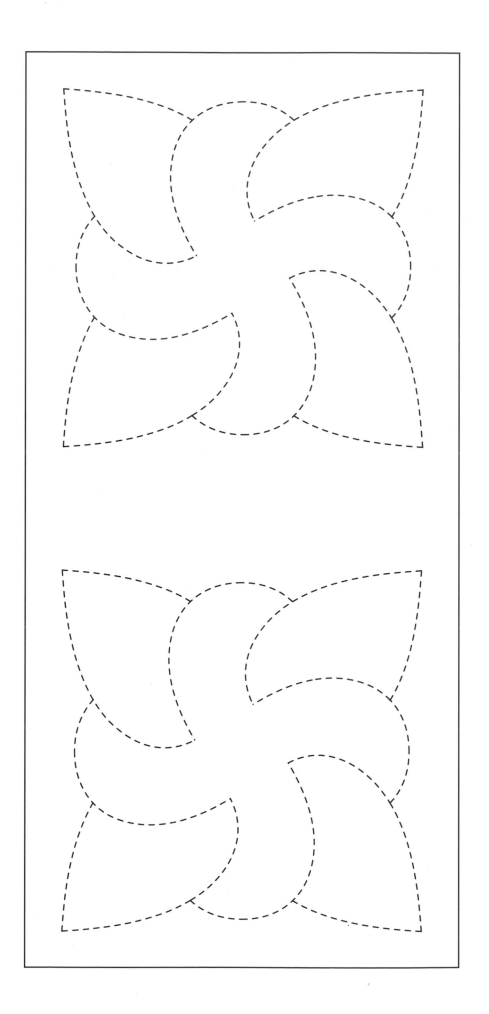

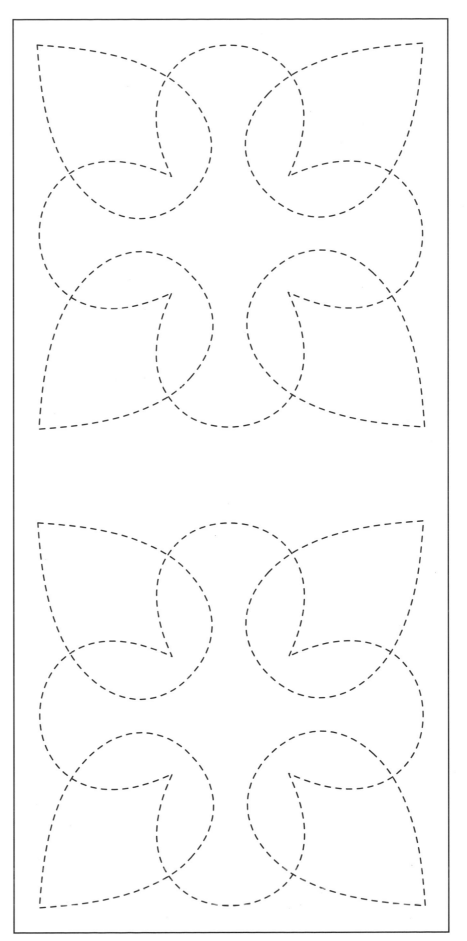

DESIGN SHOWCASE

DESIGN #66 — *page 106*

DESIGN #53— *page 94*

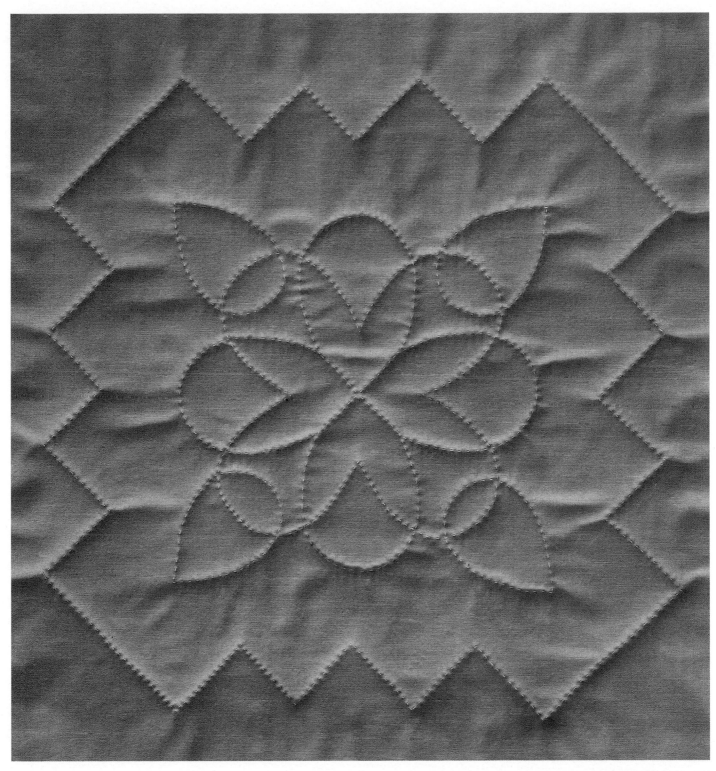

CLASSIC DESIGN—*page 150*

DESIGN #12—*page 33*

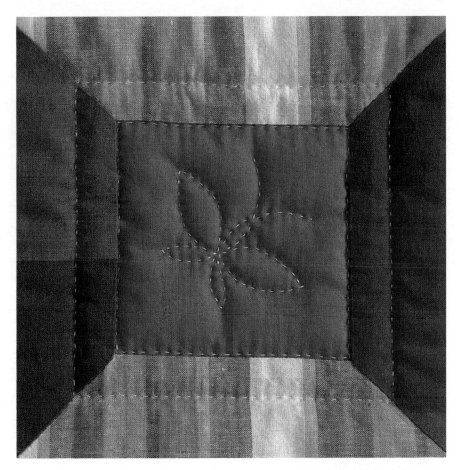

DESIGN EXTRACTION—*page 177*

DESIGN #19—*page 42*

DESIGN #25—*page 52*

DESIGN #49—*page 74*

DESIGN #24—*page 51*

FLORA AND FAUNA—page 154

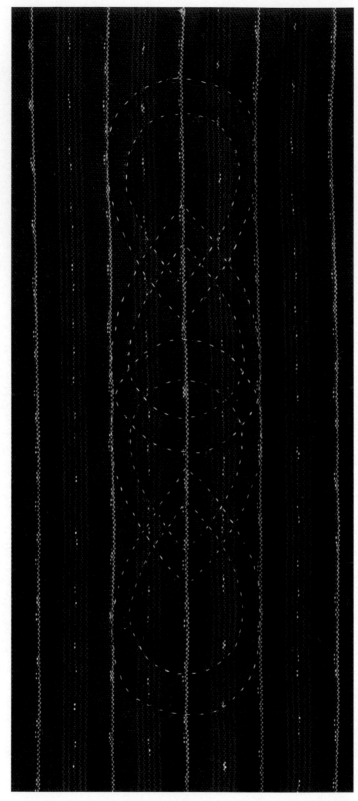

DESIGN #65—*page 105*

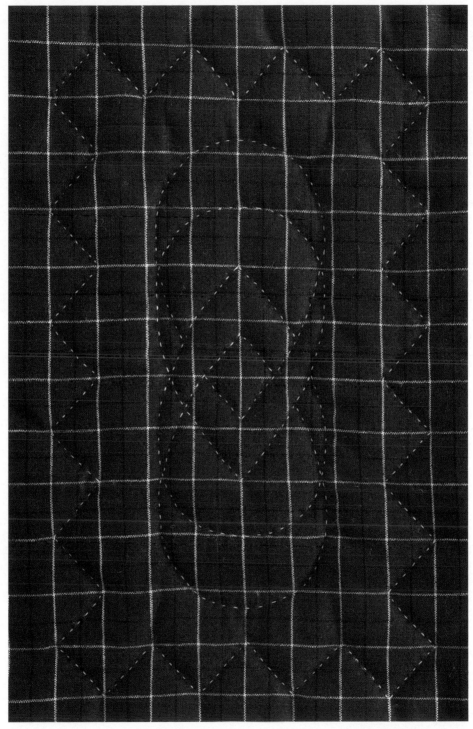

DESIGN #36—*page 64*

DESIGN #39—*on oversized pattern page*

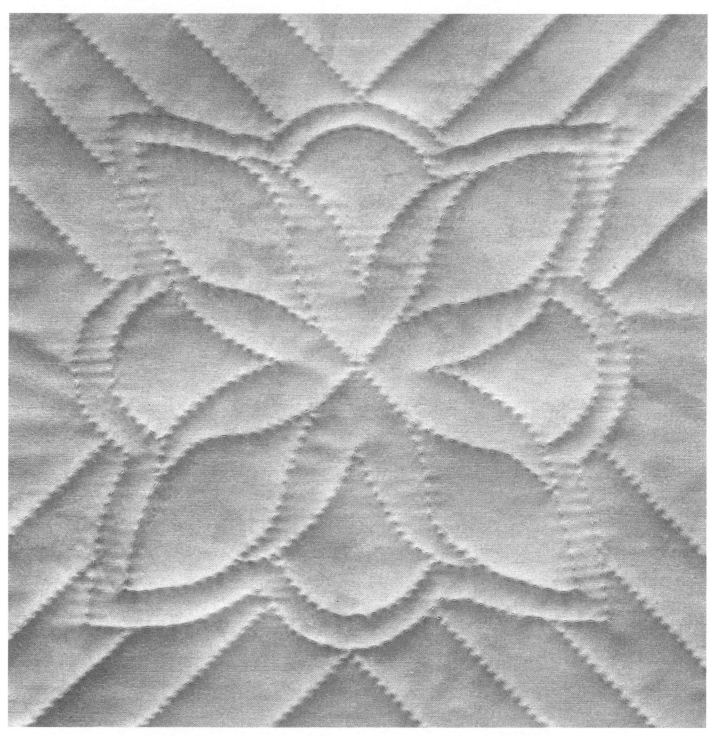

DESIGN #77—*page 123*

DESIGN #5—*page 24*

DESIGN EXTRACTION—*page 87*

DESIGN #15—*page 38*

ADDING MOTION SOLUTION—*page 181*

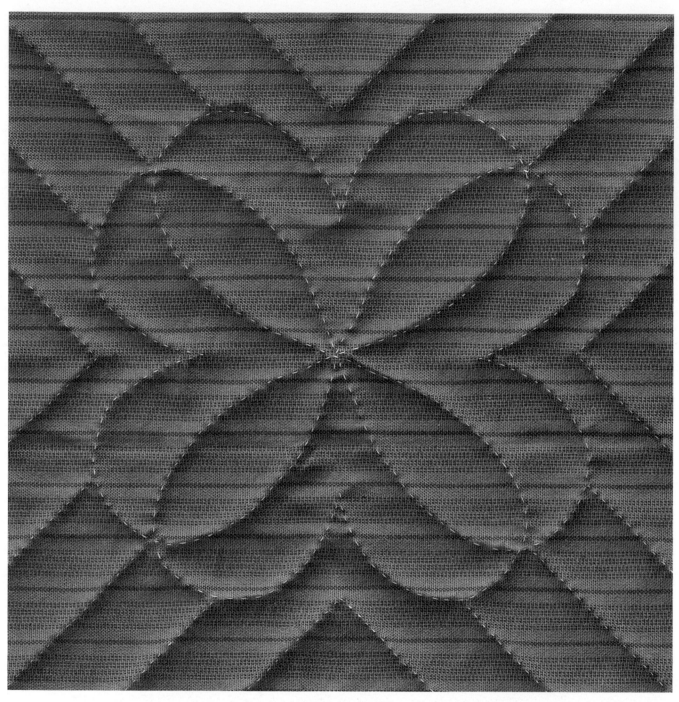

DESIGN #69—*page 111*

Portfolio

$\mathcal{T}$HIS SECTION CONTAINS 22 ready-to-use quilting designs for blocks, backgrounds, and borders. All have been created with one or more of the three simple shapes introduced at the beginning of the book—the teardrop, the heart, and the flower.

Together with the 79 designs from the preceding **Workshop** sections and the 5 border and corner patterns on the foldout pattern insert, you have a total of 106 quilting patterns in a wide range of sizes, shapes, and styles at your disposal.

Some artistic license has been exercised with the addition of design details and embellishments. Minor modifications have been made to enhance other designs.

The **Portfolio** designs are grouped in three sections:

CLASSIC DESIGNS

FLORA AND FAUNA

BEYOND THE ORDINARY

Beyond their obvious use as patterns for quilting, please regard these **Portfolio** designs as evidence of what can be generated from simple, unadorned shapes. More importantly, I hope they will serve as an inspiration for you to create your own personal designs.

Classic Designs

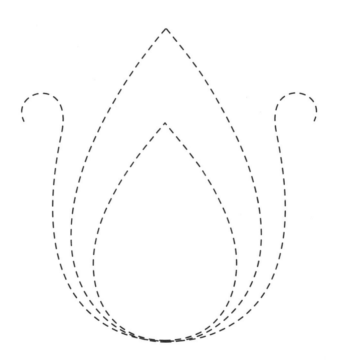

A Classic Definition

"Of recognized value," "traditional and enduring", and "simple but elegant" are some of the standard phrases in a dictionary definition of **classic.** A description that applies even more suitably to classic quilting designs is "characterized by simple tailored lines that stay in fashion year after year".

The following classic designs are marked by their simplicity, traditional appeal, and recognized value. Many others are scattered throughout this book. Glance back into the preceding **Workshop** sections for additional examples of "simple, yet elegant" classic patterns. Previous designs that would fit comfortably into our **Classic Portfolio** include #1, #3, #10, #25, #30, #34, #50, #62, #67, #68, and #75.

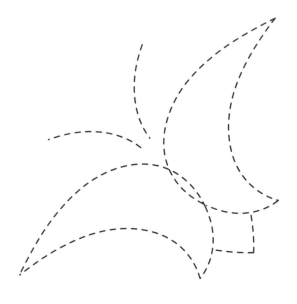

Living, Breathing Designs

The few designs included here lean heavily toward the flora—flowers, vines, and leaves—the traditionally favored quilting patterns. The arrangements and settings, however, are probably unlike any you've seen or used before.

If representational designs are your preference, I encourage you to take your pencil, paper, and teardrop template and begin your own designs. My personal portfolio of floral and faunal quilting designs is thick and heavy, full of fruit, blossoms, foliage, insects, birds, and mammals. Why not try your hand at plants, animals, and other living things? Watch for tulips, pansies, lilies, strawberries, pineapples, and pine boughs. Frogs, bugs, mice, bumblebees, and birds are all waiting to be born and set free.

Additional flora and fauna are found in the **Workshop** sections. Look for these living, breathing designs: #13, #19, #27, #28, #31, #38, #39, #42, #71, #74, #76, and #77.

Innovative or Outlandish?

The final **Portfolio** designs include what some quilters might label "unusual or downright weird". Some quilters will find these designs captivating, others will find them repugnant. Your particular personal response to these designs is not important. What is crucial is that they generate a response.

These nine designs suggest new shapes, new lines, and new directions. Each is stretching conventional design into something more singular and surprising. If you are among those that favor innovative designs, give them a try. Then look back in the **Workshop** sections for these additional **Beyond the Ordinary** designs: #5, #11, #16, #22, #35, #40, #48, #49, #52, #54, #60, and #66.

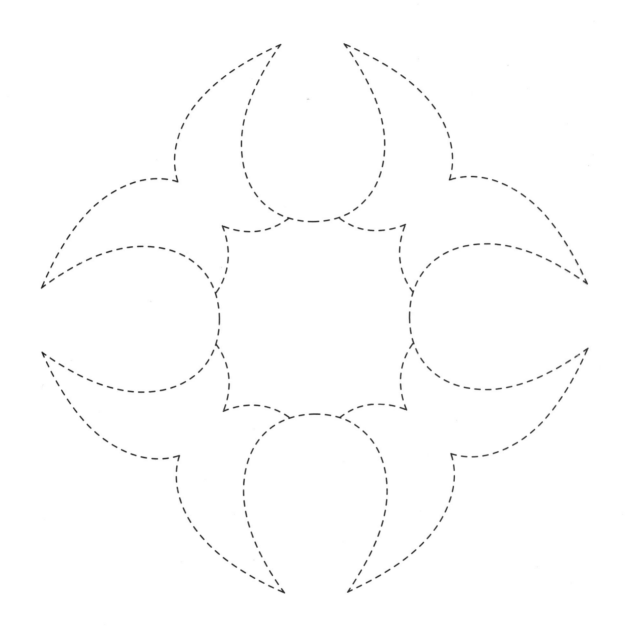

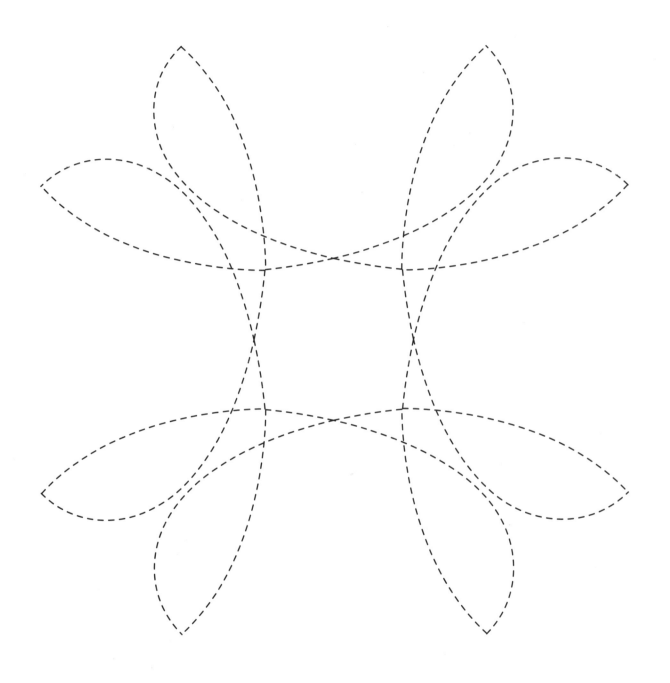

Appendices

APPENDIX A

Ten Steps for Creating Your Own Quilting Designs

Supplies: Sharp pencil, eraser, ruler, scissors, template plastic, black marking pen, and white unlined paper.

1 Examine your quilt top for the spaces that cry out for quilting, or where quilting designs can be highlighted. Search in the blocks, the background, between design areas, the latticework, the borders, and other places that might accommodate a quilted design. Define and measure these spaces that need quilting.

2 Make a paper pattern of each area. These spaces may be blocks, triangles, rectangles, or other shapes. Cut your piece of paper the same size as the area on the quilt, so you are dealing with the actual finished size.

3 Lightly mark ¼ inch (.6 cm) clearance lines, in pencil, just inside the outer edges of each space. This is to avoid placement of quilting designs in the perimeter where bulky seams may be pressed.

4 Lightly mark grid lines that bisect or divide the space into smaller workable units. Useful grid lines may include horizontal, vertical, and diagonal lines. It may be appropriate to divide a space in halves or thirds, etc. Any division to convert the space into more manageable areas is helpful.

5 Select a shape that complements the patterns in the quilt top. This may be the teardrop, heart, or flower from this book. If these are not appropriate, choose a simple shape from within the context of the appliqué or piecing.

6 Draw the selected motif and make a clear plastic template. You may opt to make additional sizes of the motif for filling very small and very large spaces on the quilt.

7 Place the design template on the paper area, experimenting to find comfortable spacing and a pleasing design. Try various techniques such as radiation from the center, reversing the template, and overlapping.

8 Add any details or filler to enhance the quilting design. Use special techniques such as adding motion or emphasizing the secondary designs.

9 Erase all unwanted design lines, grid lines, and clearance lines.

10 Highlight the completed quilting design with dark broken lines, and watch it come to life.

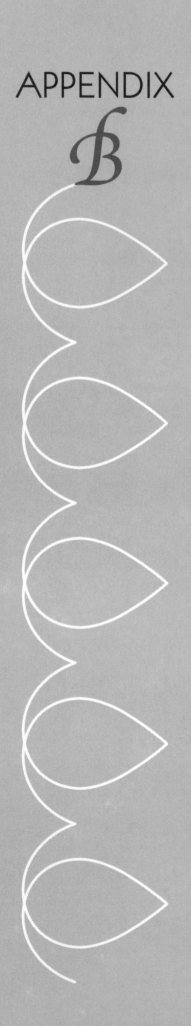

APPENDIX B

Design Extraction Examples

Some of the possible design extractions from Example B on page 90 are illustrated here. Remember, these are just some of the designs. I'm sure you found plenty of others. Remember, too, there are no wrong answers! (You shouldn't be snooping in this Appendix unless you have already read the section on **Design Extraction** on pages 77–91!)

APPENDIX

C

Solutions for NOW IT'S YOUR TURN! *Exercises*

I. *ADDING MOTION*—POSSIBLE SOLUTIONS FOR DESIGN #61

These diagrams illustrate four different line removal strategies to convert Design #61 into a rotating pattern. Perhaps you found additional ways. Refer back to pages 98–102 for the section on **Adding Motion** for instructions and exercises.

II. *CONTINUOUS LINE DESIGNS*—POSSIBLE SOLUTIONS FOR DESIGNS #71, #72, AND #73

Suggested starting and ending points, directional arrows, and stitching order are illustrated for Designs #71, #72, and #73. Don't forget, there may be several workable options. Your plan may be more sensible than mine!

Refer back to pages 109–118 in the **Continuous Line Designs** section for additional exercises and instructions for creating one-line designs.

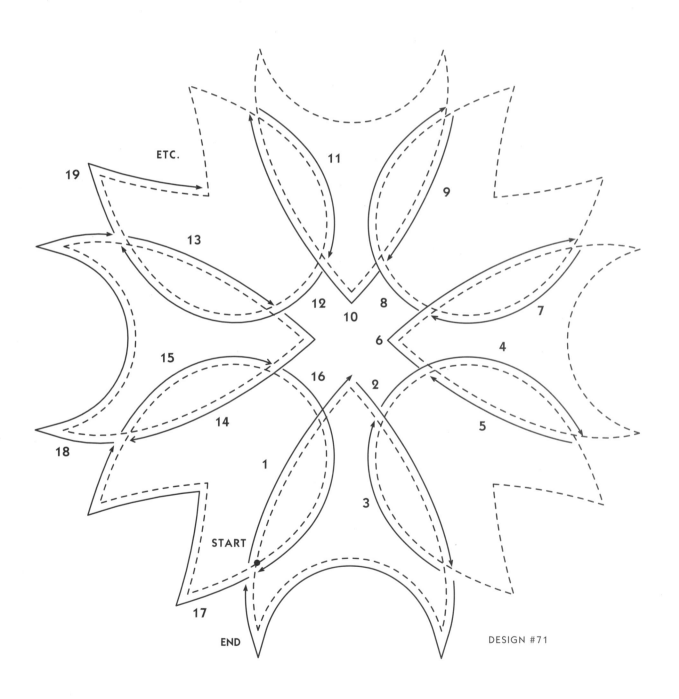

DESIGN #71

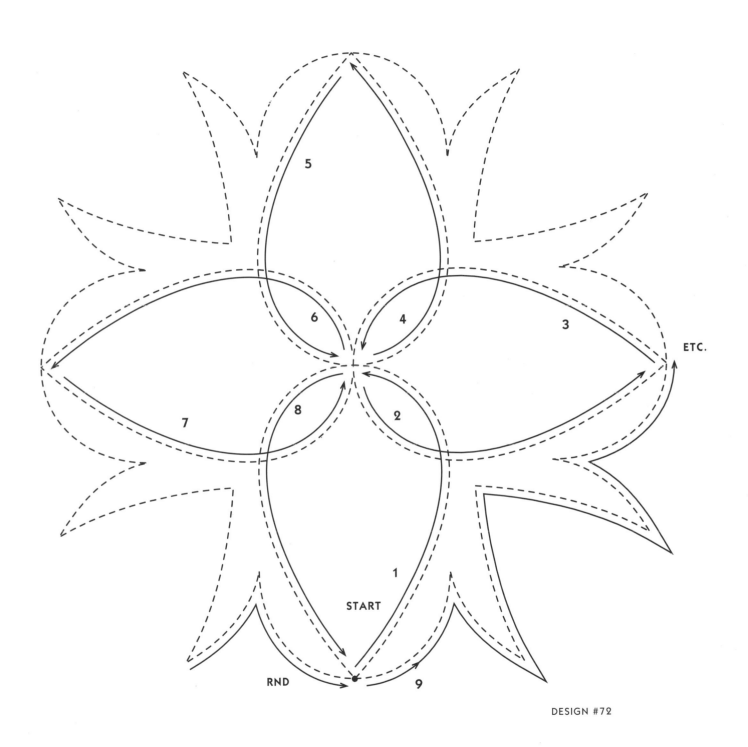

5

6 4 3 ETC.

7 8 2

1

START

RND 9

DESIGN #72

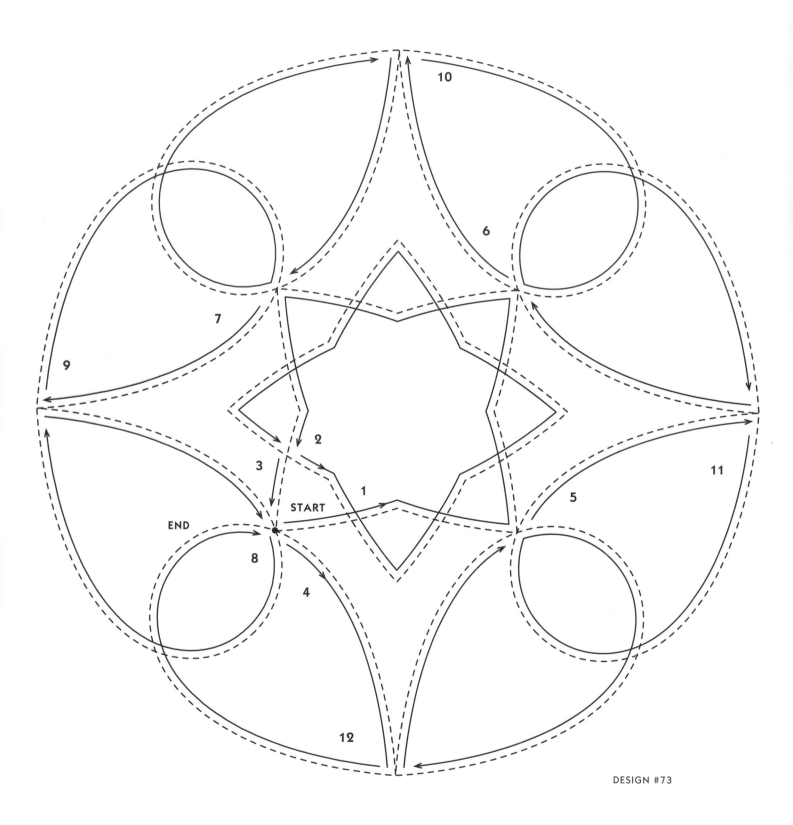

10

6

7

9

2

3

1

START

END

8

4

5

11

12

DESIGN #73

III. *TRANSFERRING DESIGNS*—POSSIBLE SOLUTIONS FOR DESIGNS #78 AND #79

Suggestions for *multiple marking templates* for Designs #78 and #79 are illustrated. Refer back to page 119–127 in the **Transferring Designs** section for complete instructions and additional exercises.

Stencil 1 for Design #78

Stencil 2 for Design #78

Stencil 1 for Design #79

Stencil 2 for Design #79: Re-position to complete the remaining inner lines.

APPENDIX

D

Metric Conversion Chart

INCHES	CENTIMETERS	INCHES	CENTIMETERS
1/8	.3	6	15.2
1/4	.6	6 1/2	16.5
1/2	1.3	7	17.8
3/4	1.9	7 1/2	19
1	2.5	8	20.3
1 1/2	3.8	8 1/2	21.6
1 3/4	4.5	9	22.9
2	5.1	9 1/2	24.1
2 1/2	6.4	10	25.4
3	7.6	11	27.9
3 1/2	8.9	12	30.5
4	10.2	13	33
4 1/2	11.4	14	35.6
5	12.7	15	38.1
5 1/2	14		

Metric Conversion Factors:

To convert inches to centimeters, multiply by 2.54 (inches x 2.54 = centimeters).
To convert centimeters to inches, multiply by 0.4 (centimeters x 0.4 = inches).

APPENDIX
Æ

Templates

FLOWER TEMPLATE

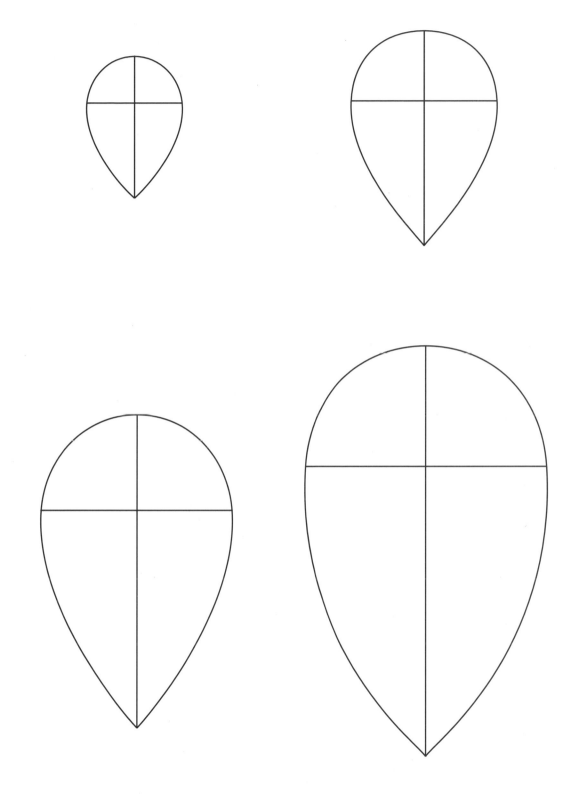

TEARDROP TEMPLATES

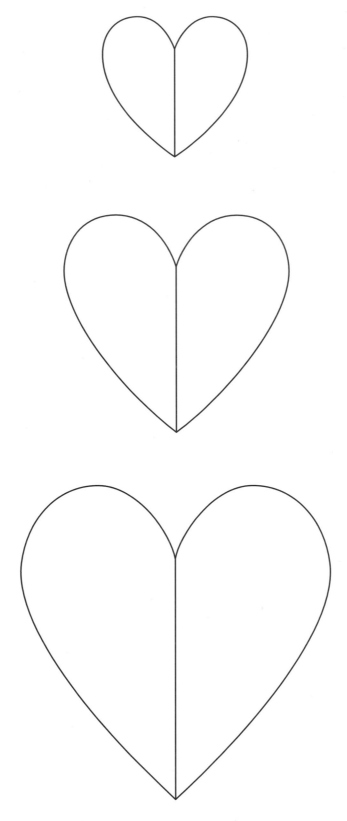

HEART TEMPLATES

Author's Profile

THE IMAGE OF JUDY FLORENCE skating in graceful quilting loops and swirls as she glides over the ice offers a delightful metaphor for her design creativity. From the solitude of a winter landscape to involvement with students' projects, Judy moves easily from the creative experience to practical application in the classroom.

Her popular workshops centering on quilting designs are renowned for the originality and creativity she inspires in her students. Judy's teaching credentials include prominent conferences and guilds throughout the United States, as well as symposia in Australia, Canada and Scotland. In 1994, as the quiltmaking representative of a cultural delegation to Chiba, Japan, Judy taught and displayed her quilts to an enthusiastic audience. Her academic background comprises a B.A. in Liberal Arts, a B.S. in Home Economics and an M.S. in Adult Education, all from the University of Wisconsin.

In addition to widespread teaching and exhibiting, Judy is the prolific author of nine books: *Award-Winning Quilts and How to Make Them; Award-Winning Quilts and How to Make Them, Book II; Award-Winning Scrap Quilts; Award-Winning Quick Quilts; A Collection of Favorite Quilts: Narratives, Patterns and Directions for 15 Quilts; More Projects & Patterns: A Second Collection of Favorite Quilts; Scrap Quilts and How to make Them; Quick Quilts: Patterns and Techniques;* and *Creative Designs for Hand and Machine Quilting.* She is also the author of numerous articles, illustrated with her quilts and designs, which have appeared frequently in leading periodicals, including "Quilter's Newsletter Magazine", "The American Quilter", and "Quilting Today".

Judy has extended her winter exercise and design program by taking up in-line skating. Glimpses of her creative process in action may be seen on the ponds and streets of Eau Claire, Wisconsin, where she lives with her husband and two sons.

APPENDIX

DESIGN #41

DESIGN #41 BORDER

DESIGN #38 BORDER